MARBURGER GEOGRAPHISCHE SCHRIFTEN

Herausgeber: C. Schott
Schriftleiter: A. Pletsch

Heft 97

Claudia Notzke

Indian Reserves in Canada
Development Problems of the Stoney and Peigan Reserves in Alberta

Marburg/Lahn 1985

Im Selbstverlag des Geographischen Instituts der Universität Marburg

ISSN 0341-9290
ISBN 3-88353-021-2

Acknowledgements

I should like to thank my supervisor, Dr. Lynn Rosenvall, and my committee, Nelson Gutnick of the Faculty of Social Welfare and Drs. Larry Cordes of the Department of Geography and Donald Smith of the Department of History, for their interest, advice and encouragement throughout this project.

Many thanks are extended to Chief Nelson Small Legs Sr. and the Peigan Band Council, and to Chief Frank Powderface, Chief John Snow and Chief Bill Ear and the Stoney Band Council for their permission to conduct this study on their reserves. Cooperation and support provided by individual council members and administration staff on both reserves is most gratefully acknowledged.

I am also indebted to my research assistants during a socio-economic sample survey in both communities, Doreen Kootenay of the Stoneys and Teresa Pard of the Peigan, without whose patience and tact this survey would not have been possible. Thanks go out to all those band members who kindly provided the requested information.

This research was supported by a Government of Canada Award, a teaching assistantship from the Department of Geography, and a Thesis Research Grant from the University of Calgary.

Special thanks are extended to the Canadian Embassy in Bonn for funding this publication.

Claudia Notzke

The present volume is the unabridged version of the author's thesis, entitled "The Development of Canadian Indian Reserves as illustrated by the Example of the Stoney and Peigan Reserves" submitted to the Faculty of Graduate Studies of the University of Calgary (Dept. of Geography) in August 1982 in partial fulfillment of the requirements for the Degree of Doctor of Philosophy.

Contents

	page
Acknowledgements	IV
Contents	V
List of Tables	VI
List of Figures	VI
Chapter 1: Introduction	1
1.1 Identification of the Problem and Objective of the Study	1
1.2 The Land and the People	2
1.3 Review of Literature	2
1.4 Research Procedure, Limitations and Assumptions	5
Chapter 2: Traditional Life and Economy	6
Chapter 3: Treaty Number Seven and early Reserve Days	10
Chapter 4: Aspirations for the Future	19
Chapter 5: The Land-based Economy	23
5.1 The physical-geographical Conditions	23
5.1.1 Topography	23
5.1.2 Climate	23
5.1.3 Soils	28
5.1.4 Vegetation	30
5.1.5 Geology	34
5.2 The Factors of Production: Land, Labour and Capital	35
5.2.1 The Land	36
5.2.1.1 Land: an unresolved Issue	36
5.2.1.2 Land: Quantity and Tenure System	47
5.2.2 The People	54
5.2.2.1 Demography	54
5.2.2.2 Education	57
5.2.2.3 Labour Force: occupational Structure and economic and cultural Outlook	63
5.2.3 The Capital	66
5.2.3.1 The economic Situation of Stoney and Peigan Households	66
5.2.3.2 Band Funds	67
5.2.3.3 Potential outside Sources of Funding	68
5.3 The renewable Resource Sector: Potential and economic Activities	71
5.3.1 Livestock Production	71
5.3.2 Dryland Farming	79
5.3.3 Irrigation Farming	80
5.3.4 Forestry	81
5.3.5 Outdoor Recreation	85
5.4 The non-renewable Resource Sector: Potential and economic Activities	89
Chapter 6: Settlement Pattern and Communication Network	91
Chapter 7: The Manufacturing and Servicing Sector	94
7.1 Secondary Industries	94
7.2 Service Industries	95
Chapter 8: Conclusion and Outlook: The Peigan and Stoney Reserves as "underdeveloped" Areas and "internal Colonies"	97
Bibliography	101

List of Tables

		page
1	Description of the Forest Land on the Morley Reserve	82
2	Stocked Forest Area in Hectar by Cover Type and Cutting Class	83

List of Figures

1	Regional Setting of the Reserves	3
2	Tribal Distribution a) before 1730 b) after 1730	7
3	The Location of the Kootenay Plains and the Treaty Areas	12
4	Mean monthly Temperature and Precipitation 1931-1960 for selected Centres in southern Alberta	24
5	Average Water Balance: Lethbridge, Alberta	26
6	Climatograph: Wheat Yield (bushels per acre) after Summer Fallow, 1908-1970	27
7	Peigan Reserve: Soil Capability for Agriculture	29
8	Morley Reserve: Distribution of Grassland and Forest Land	31
9	Sections to illustrate various Types of structural Traps favourable to the Accumulation of Oil and Gas	35
10	The Bighorn-Kootenay Plains Land Claim	40
11	The Composition of Stoney Land	42
12	Peigan Reserve: Areas (recently or presently) subject to Dispute	45
13	Peigan Reserve: Land Tenure	50
14	Peigan Reserve: Leased Land	51
15	Peigan Reserve: Land under Cultivation	52
16	Morley Reserve: Land Tenure	54
17	Population Pyramids for the Peigan and Stoney Samples	57

Chapter 1

Introduction

1.1 Identification of the Problem and Objective of the Study

Looking at Canada as a whole, approximately 74 per cent of the country's status Indians live in 561 bands on their 2,281 reserves and 85 "crown land" settlements. There are about two dozen reserves within or adjacent to cities (such as Caughnawaga near Montreal or the Sarcee outside Calgary), but generally speaking, the reserves are rural, very small, and scattered across the country. A common characteristic of Canadian Indian reserves (and rural communities of non-status Indians and Metis as well) is the fact that - to a varying degree - they do not have the resources and/or the infrastructure to economically sustain their ever increasing population. They constitute patches of a "third world environment" within the framework of a western industrialized nation. As an analytical aid Davis (1968: 220) suggests to view the reserve situation within a broader frame of reference: the exploitive relationship prevailing between metropolis and hinterland. This idea is not new, but what needs to be emphasized today, according to this author, is the point that "the metropolis not only exploits its hinterlands, it creates them, and perpetuates as long as possible their economic, social and political dependence". The analogy drawn by another writer, Carstens (1971: 129), is very similar in its implications: "The Indians of Canada who are under the Indian Act and live within the economic, social, and territorial confines of reserves are not wards of the government as some have argued; they are members of little colonies within the borders of the dominating nation." Carstens goes so far as to classify reserve communities as "peasantry" (as Kroeber coined this socio-economic term) - rural people living in relation to market towns, provided we see them as consisting of class segments of a population that contains urban centres. With regard to many cultural and social implications one cannot but question such statement, since North American Indians simply do not adhere to a primary peasant culture, and the contact situation did not imprint itself on a tabula rasa; yet with regard to the key concept of peasantry, i.e. dependence, there is indeed a striking analogy. Moreover, the author calls our attention to another significant feature of reserves: "Reserves are social systems which have been ossified by the economic and political systems on which they are dependent."

Whatever analogy we apply to the situation, it becomes evident that Indian reserves possess a very distinct geography of their own. At the same time, Canadian (and United States) Indian reserves are virtually untouched by geographers. This is surprising, since, geography being a synthesizing discipline, geographers appear to be particularly equipped to deal with development problems such as those presenting themselves on reserves. Experience has shown (Deprez, no date; Deprez and Sigurdson, 1969) that strategies based on the so-called bottleneck conception - focusing on just one component of the problem such as education - are of no avail. The situation calls for a much broader approach which deals simultaneously with physical and human development, and which above all takes into account all those factors, which render development problems of Indian reserves somewhat different from the ones encountered by other areas within the province subject to regional disparity. It has been repeatedly confirmed to me by Indian people from the Peigan and Stoney Reserves that it is this broad and synthesizing approach and the attempt to view the situation from within, what they will be looking for in the final result.

Therefore, my focus will differ somewhat from most of the few studies done so far of Indian reserves by individuals or, more commonly, agencies. Employees of consultant companies or government agencies simply lack the conditioning and the necessary time to adopt anything but the same approach they would use in white communities. Hence most studies appear to be mere physical resource assessments under a somewhat ethnocentric perspective. They do not take into account the cultural, social and political realities of the Indian people and the "reserve situation". I would like to focus my interest on questions like the following: What is the Indian (particularly the Stoney and Peigan) concept of "progress" and "development"? Is it an alternative to the concept white society is accustomed to? How have Indian people proceeded since self-government in order to realize their ideas and to achieve their goals? What kind of problems have been encountered? How do Indians manage to culturally accommodate inevitable changes, and how does economic development accommodate pre-existing cultural traits?

1.2   The Land and the People

The reserves which are subject to this study, the Stoney and the Peigan Reserves, are located in southern Alberta, in an area encompassing the largest Indian reserves in Canada (Fig. 1). The Stoney Indians inhabit three reserves, all of which are situated in the foothills of the Rocky Mountains. The Morley Reserve - which is the main reserve - is centred around the township or Morley which is roughly 56 kilometres (35 miles) west of Calgary. It comprises 460 square kilometres (178 square miles) and includes those reserves, number 142, 143, and 144 that make up the main block and Rabbit Lake Reserve 142 B, comprising some 67 square kilometres (26 square miles), 16 kilometres (10 miles) to the north of Morley proper. These areas centre around the Bow River. The Trans-Canada Highway No. 1, Highway No. 1 A and the Canadian Pacific Railways Transcontinental main line, coincide with the east-west axis of the reserve. The Eden Valley Reserve is situated on the Highwood River. It comprises only 18 square kilometres (7 square miles) and is composed of two separate areas, Eden Valley proper and Hughes Ranch on the Pekisko Creek. The most northerly of the three reserves is the Bighorn Reserve on the northwest bank of the North Saskatchewan River, it comprises 20 square kilometres (8 square miles). Each reserve thus is situated in a river valley with undulating terrain at a general elevation of 1,370 metres (4,495 feet) above sea level. The total population is 2,296.

The Peigan occupy two reserves in the southwestern corner of the province. The main reserve number 147 is centred around Brocket which is 80 kilometres (50 miles) southwest of Lethbridge. It comprises 423.5 square kilometres (163.5 square miles) and is located on the Oldman River, near the foot of the Porcupine Hills. Highway No. 3 and the Canadian Pacific Railways Crowsnest Pass - Lethbridge line run diagonally through the reserve from northeast to southwest. In addition there is a 28 square kilometres (11 square miles) forest reserve, some 32 kilometres (20 miles) to the northwest of Brocket, a square block known as the Timber Limit or reserve number 147 B, set in the Porcupine Hills. The Peigan population numbers 1,812.

Historically, the Peigan and Stoney Reserves are Treaty Seven reserves. This treaty, the so-called Blackfoot Treaty, was the seventh in a series of eleven, and was signed at Blackfoot Crossing in 1877 between the Crown and the native tribes occupying the area that today is southern Alberta: the Stoneys, the Sarcee, the Peigan, Blood and Blackfoot proper. These five groups now inhabit reserves in their former homeland. The Treaty Seven reserves share a common history and their location in a province presently undergoing an economic boom, but they have been subject to quite different courses of development, due to differences in their culture, endowment with natural resources, in their leadership and local policy, and their dealings with provincial and federal government. Due to the discovery of natural gas on their land the Stoneys may be considered a relatively wealthy tribe, whereas the Peigan depend on a very narrow resource base, namely land and water. This basic difference is modified by a variety of other physical and human factors.

1.3   Review of Literature

Information on the early reserve period of the Stoney and Peigan is scarce, even more so than for the Blood and Blackfoot, where anthropological studies of the adaptation to a reserve situation were conducted. The first, which was done by E. S. Goldfrank, is entitled "Changing Configurations in the Social Organiz-

Figure 1: Regional Setting of the Reserves

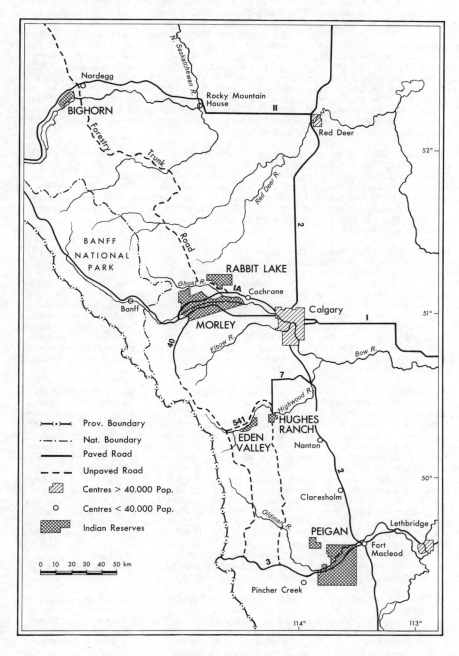

Sources: Prov. of Alberta, Official Road Map 1980/81; Map 82 H Series A 502 C.N.

ation of a Blackfoot Tribe during the Reserve Period" (New York, 1945); the second by L.M. and J. Hanks is "Tribe under Trust, a Study of the Blackfoot Reserve of Alberta" (University of Toronto Press, 1950). Both studies show that each reserve has to be looked at individually. Despite a similar cultural and historical background of the three tribes of the Blackfoot "Confederacy" they are likely to have undergone quite dissimilar developments after the conclusion of Treaty Seven, and generalizations may be highly misleading. In his book "These Mountains are our Sacred Places. The Story of the Stoney Indians" (Toronto and Sarasota, 1977) Chief John Snow writes to some extent about the evolution of his reserve, drawing on oral traditions of his people and government files. The same sources will be used for this study: The Annual Reports of the Department of Indian Affairs (starting in 1880 when the Department of Indian Affairs was set up as an independent department) yield reports by Indian Agencies and the Superintendency; and some oral information is available from Indian individuals.

The year 1966 witnessed the release of the Hawthorn Report (Hawthorn, H.B. ed., A Survey of the Contemporary Indians of Canada. Economic, Political, Educational Needs and Policies. In two Volumes. Indian Affairs Branch Ottawa, 1966). It constitutes an extensive examination of the conduct of Indian affairs that had been commissioned by the Department of Indian Affairs and Northern Development (before 1966 the Indian Affairs Branch of the Department of Citizenship and Immigration) in 1963. Due to its favourable echo in the Indian community it deserves further attention in Chapter 4.

In 1977 the Indian Association of Alberta submitted a "Joint N.I.B./D.I.A.N.D. Socio-Economic Study for the Alberta Region". This study contains a generalized appraisal of socio-economic conditions of Alberta's Indian population and a series of band profiles. A similar study was prepared by the Research Branch of The Indian and Inuit Affairs Program (of the Department of Indian Affairs and Northern development) in 1980, "An Overview of Demographic, Social and Economic Conditions among Alberta's registered Indian Population". The same year witnessed the release of "Indian Conditions. A Survey", also compiled by the Department of Indian Affairs and Northern Development. This publication, while much more limited in scope and detail than the Hawthorn Report, documents principal developments and trends in the social, economic and political conditions of Indians in Canada and highlights changes since the 1950s.

In contrast to the Peigan Reserve the Stoneys have previously attracted the attention of university-based researchers. The only geographical work was done by R.E. England in the 1960s, and constitutes "A Partial Study of the Resource Potential of the Stony Indian Reservation: Livestock and Forest Enterprises". England's thesis is a pure physical resource assessment, and the author explicitly states: "The grazing and forest potential of the reserve has been calculated assuming conditions of optimum management. Whether or not all management procedures can be applied, because of cultural or legislative difficulties, is not considered in this study." Apart from this study research has mainly been conducted in the fields of anthropology and to lesser degree, history: Munroe (1969) studied Stoney social structure; Medicine (mid-60s) examined Stoney use of "Indian Medicine"; Getty and Larner (1972) carried out a research report under the direction of the Stoney Band Council, which was to serve as an historical documentation of the Wesley Band's claims to land in the Kootenay Plains area. Getty (1974) researched "Perception as an Agent of socio-cultural Change for the Stoney Indians of Alberta". This work is best described as a history of the Stoney people from the Stoney point of view. The most recent study was conducted by Scott-Brown (1977) and is a thesis on Stoney ethnobotany.

In 1969 the Department of Indian Affairs and Northern Development contracted with the consulting firm of Underwood, McLellan and Associates Limited, to undertake two studies, The Stoney Land Use Study and The Stoney Recreational Development Study. Both these reports deal with the most efficient and effective use of reserve land but fail to take into account certain social, cultural and political realities with the result that many of the recommendations are unrealistic and would not be implemented in the ways or the areas suggested by the reports. Two similar studies were conducted for the Peigan Reserve: "An Evaluation of the Potential of the Peigan Indian Reserve" by F.E. Price and Associates Limited in 1967, and "A Study of Resource Development Requirements for the Peigan Band" by Stanley Associates Engineering Limited and McKinnon, Allen and Associates Limited in 1972. Another potential source of useful information, the Oldman River Basin Study, Phase Two. Social Impact Assessment, by P. Boothroyd and Co-West Associates in 1978 excluded the Peigan Reserve. The tense situation due to a land dispute between the Peigan Band and the Province of Alberta regarding the Lethbridge Northern Irrigation District system made it seem inappropriate for the fieldworkers to proceed with interviewing on the reserve at that time.

1.4 Research Procedure, Limitations and Assumptions

General physical geographical data as well as recommendations for farming, ranching and forestry for the regions the reserves are part of are available through sources like the Meteorological Branch of the Department of Transport, the Alberta Soil Survey, the Canada Land Inventory, the Alberta Department of Lands and Forests, the Canada Department of Agriculture and its research stations and the Alberta Department of Agriculture.

Where information has to be newly acquired, it is evident from what was outlined above, that this can only be accomplished in close cooperation with members of both reserve communities. A couple of years ago Vine Deloria Jr. (1969) wrote that the time would come when the Indian people "... will finally awaken and push the parasitic scholars off the reservations and set up realistic guidelines by which they can control what is written and said about them". That day has come for Canadian Indian reserves. Many Indian leaders feel that researchers have indulged in esoteric research and analysis with the primary purpose of advancing their personal standing within the academic community, and further that much of this research has been inaccurate and misleading. Today Indians are only interested in research that they can use as ammunition in the struggle to bring about desired changes. I agreed right from the start to close cooperation, to a mutual trade-off by making my experience and training available to them in exchange for their cooperation in gathering the material I needed, access to files, tapes, reports etc. I believe that research should be relevant to the people I am depending on to conduct it, and moreover, this association has been a great learning experience for me.

I was in constant contact with individual resource persons like cultural researchers, land claims researchers, program managers, various committees, the research department of the Stoney Reserve, Chief(s) and Council on both reserves, and some faculty members of the Native American Studies Department at the University of Lethbridge. I visited individual and band enterprises and attended council sessions, band meetings and workshops. On both reserves I conducted a socioeconomic sample survey, covering topics such as demographic and social characteristics of the population, housing situation, landuse and economic activities. The survey technique chosen was interviewing. This is virtually the only method, where a reasonable response rate can be expected, as some people are illiterate, and most are not used to dealing with written material. The interviewing activity enabled me to establish personal contact, to attune myself to the variety of people encountered, rephrase questions and give additional encouragement and reassurance. On both reserves I was accompanied by an Indian research assistant, a member of the community, who would introduce me and interpret, if necessary. It was originally intended to draw a random sample, using the band lists as a sampling frame. Due to occasional difficulty of meeting people at home, however, I decided it would be unwise to exclude people in advance; therefore, I chose a non-probability method. We would drive a random route, taking care to cover the reserve lands adequately without bias. This seemed to be an appropriate method to cover a representative cross-section of the population. On the Peigan Reserve I interviewed sixty households, constituting roughly twenty per cent of the total. With the Stoneys I conducted thirty-two interviews, thereby covering twenty-three per cent of the Chiniki Band (one of the three bands on the reserve). I originally intended to complete the same number of interviews as with the Peigan, but due to some family problems of my research assistant, and also because the results were fairly homogeneous, I was satisfied with less.

Chapter 2

Traditional Life and Economy

Unlike the aboriginal population of the United States the Canadian Indians never had to undergo the wholesale dislocation from their ancestral lands and the allocation of reserves which they would have to share with culturally different and often hostile tribes. Accordingly the Stoneys and the Peigan inhabit reserves that form small sections of their tribal homeland; the reserve populations constitute culturally homogeneous groups.

Looking further back in time though, both tribes are immigrants on the northwestern plains from the east. The Peigan are a member of the so-called Blackfoot Confederation, which belongs to the Algonkian linguistic family. For more than two centuries the three Blackfoot tribes have been known by their separate names. They are the Peigan or Pikuni, the Blood or Kainai and the Blackfoot proper or Siksika, often referred to as the Northern Blackfoot, to distinguish them from the other two tribes. Those three tribes were politically independent. But they spoke the same language, shared the same customs (with the exception of a few ceremonial rituals), intermarried, and made war upon common enemies. At present the Peigan tribe is divided into two divisions, the North Peigan in Alberta (Aputoksi Pikuni) and the South Peigan in Montana (Amiskapi Pikuni). Although they still considered themselves Peigan, they were in the final stages of separation when the treaties stopped the natural political evolution. Together the Peigan, Blood and Blackfoot proper comprised the strongest military power on the northwestern plains in historic buffalo days.

The movement of the Blackfoot Confederation onto the plains of Alberta and Montana was reconstructed by Lewis (1941) after historical evidence (Fig. 2): About 1730 the Peigan, as the frontier tribe of the Blackfoot, were on the plains of the Eagle Hills in Saskatchewan, a distance of over 640 kilometres (400 miles) from the Rocky Mountains. Presumably the Blood and Siksika were to the north and east. Within the short period from 1730 to 1745 the tribal locations in the northern plains were changed. The Blackfoot received their first horses from the Shoshone around 1730 as well as obtaining firearms and iron from the Cree and Assiniboine. Thus armed with the gun and iron for their arrows, aided by a small-pox epidemic among the Shoshone, and under pressure from the Cree and Assiniboine, the Blackfoot defeated the Shoshone in the 1730s, and initiated a period of great expansion to the west and southwest. They drove the Snakes (a Shoshone tribe) and Kutenai (Kootenay) west of the mountains. The Peigan as the frontier tribe took possession of the Bow River, and south along the foothills. The Blood came to the present Red Deer River, and the Siksika to the upper waters of the Battle River, south of Edmonton. Still another great movement of the Blackfoot took place about 1750-1770. This was the southern extension from the Bow River as far south as the upper waters of the Missouri. The reasons for this expansion were probably to obtain horses from the Flathead, and to find better buffalo country. They now controlled the whole country along the eastern foot of the Rockies, well into Saskatchewan, from the headwaters of the Missouri in the south to the North Saskatchewan River in the north. Their travels and war expeditions extended even farther.

As it is evident from these major changes in tribal habitat, it was not their direct association with whites that created modifications among the plainsmen, but rather the acquisition in protohistoric times of the horse, the gun and other implements of metal. All these reached the Plains Indians before Europeans had physically penetrated the area. The pre-horse period is usually referred to as the "dog

Figure 2: Tribal Distribution (after Lewis, 1941)
a) before 1730, b) after 1730

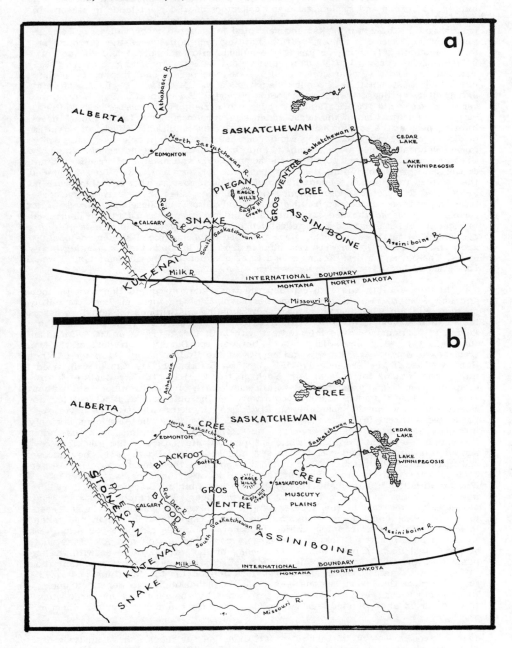

Sources: Adapted from Wormington (1965), Fig. 90

days" (or Pedestrian Culture Period, Ewers 1955), since the dog was the Indian's only domesticated animal and only beast of burden. These pedestrian Indians were hunters of buffalo and smaller game and collectors of wild plant foods in season. In quest of buffalo they wandered the plains, carrying their possessions by dog travois and on their own backs, and retreated to timbered river valleys or to marginal forested areas in winter. Buffalo hunting techniques were the surround on foot, impounding (driving or luring the animals into enclosures) and the use of buffalo jumps (chasing buffalo over cliffs or cut-banks). According to Ewers (1955) many of the traits so characteristic of the historic period had deep roots in the prehistoric past, such as the basic dependence on the buffalo for food, clothing and shelter; teepees; travois; the foot war party; the coup; the Sun Dance; the camp circle; men's societies and a circumscribed range with summer and winter camps. The acquisition of the horse added a pastoral component to the life of these hunting people; the feeding habits of horses further conditioned Blackfoot nomadism, originally only controlled by the wandering habits of their staple food source, the bison. Materially, they were enriched, and, in general, the standard of living rose. Greater ease of transport permitted the accumulation and hauling of greater amounts of material goods, including items not essential for survival. Swift horses enabled the hunters to approach distant herds of buffalo almost at will, and they were no longer tied to suitable topographic locations for drive sites. The surround on horseback and buffalo-running (pursuit of individual animals on horseback) largely if not completely replaced the use of pounds and buffalo jumps. Social groups increased in size through the merging of pedestrian bands, partly in the interests of self-protection. With these increased numbers more elaborate social structures could grow and flourish. Women were emancipated from the arduous task of packing heavy loads. The old and infirm no longer had to be abandoned. The accumulation of wealth (in terms of horses and goods) gave rise to a class system.

In the late 18th and 19th century the fur trade, in conjunction with the horse and new weapons, was to become another revolutionizing force in Blackfoot culture change, and far from breaking down their existing institutions, it acted as a stimulus to their development. Due to their extensive habitat the Blackfoot - and the Peigan in particular - came into contact with both the American and the Canadian fur trade (1). After sporadic contacts between the Blackfoot, traders of the Montreal-based Northwest Company and agents of the Hudson's Bay Company (Anthony Henday 1754, Henry Pressick 1760/61, Matthew Cocking 1772), who in vain tried to induce the Indians to trade at Fort York on Hudson Bay, trading posts of both companies were finally established within easy reach of the Blackfoot. But without exception these Canadian trading posts were on the outskirts of Blackfoot territory, mostly along the North Saskatchewan River, and therefore the traders never represented a threat in the eyes of the Indians. In contrast the Americans not only intruded right into Blackfoot country, but rather than depending upon the Indian fur supply they sent their own white trappers. Quite naturally the Blackfoot resented this intrusion and competition and attacked them. Up to 1831, they successfully prevented the establishment of trading posts in their territory in the United States. After that the American Fur Company adopted the Canadian system of trading with the Indians, and Fort Mackenzie was built in Blackfoot territory. By now the hey-day of the Canadian fur trade was over. The supply of beaver was almost exhausted east of the Rockies, and the Hudson's Bay Company was forced to introduce methods of conservation. But in any case only the Peigan had taken to large scale beaver trapping, while the other two tribes did not. For a long time the fur trade with the Blackfoot had largely consisted of wolf and fox skins, both of which had been trapped before the coming of the whites. However with the expansion of the fur trade the plains tribes had come to play a very important though different role, namely as the chief providers of food for the far-flung posts. The fur traders of the forest regions above the North Saskatchewan depended upon those posts which were supplied with provisions by the Blackfoot for large quantities of dried and pounded meat, pemmican, backfat and dried berries. The Ca-

---

1) For a comparison of the American and Canadian fur trade and an analysis of its impact on Blackfoot culture, see Lewis, O., 1941, The Effects of White Contact upon Blackfoot Culture with special Reference to the Role of the Fur Trade, University of Washington Press, Seattle and London.

nadian fur trade also provided the Blackfoot with a market for horses, which were needed to transport supplies by land to the outlying posts. The establishment of the American traders in Blackfoot territory coincided with the displacement of the beaver trade by that of buffalo hides, which had its greatest development in the United States. In addition, there was an extensive trade in tongues and tallow. But whatever the mode of exchange was, Blackfoot economy, in contrast to the tribes to the east and west, never became subservient to that of the whites for its subsistence needs. However, with the infiltration of some labor saving devices of white material culture, and the consequent rise in the standard of living, the luxuries soon became necessities, and Blackfoot dependence upon the whites, though on a different level than that of the Cree or Kutenai, was no less real. Other changes in tribal society came about as a result of the Indians' increased efforts to procure more buffalo, their frequent visits of the forts and their increased material wealth. Examples for culture change would be the expansion of polygnyny and an ensuing increase in the size of horse herds; a stimulation of intertribal intercourse and resultant cultural exchange; effects on the authority of the chiefs, and considerable changes in the character and purpose of warfare. Social stratification was even more enhanced, and individualism flourished.

Many of the developments recounted here also apply to the Stoneys although they seem to have been exposed more marginally to both the introduction of the horse on a large scale and the fur trade. The Stoneys or Assiniboine (Chippewa for "one who cooks by the use of stones") were originally part of the large Sioux Nation, or, more distinctly, of the Yanktonai. Judging from the slight dialectical difference in the language their separation from their parent stem cannot have greatly preceded the appearance of the European (Hodge 1913: 45). When the Jesuit missions were established at Lake Superior in the 1640s, Sioux and Assiniboine were already bitter enemies - "the sort of enmity that marks family feuds" (Laurie 1957/59: 3).

Looking at the reserves located in the Albertan foothills we are interested in a particular group of this people: Mountain Stoneys, Mountain Assiniboine or Swampy Ground Assiniboine are but some of the various names given to them in the course of history. While the Assiniboine in general became known as typical adherents to the plains and buffalo culture, and in fact shared many characteristics with the tribes of the Blackfoot Confederation, this group consisted of wood dwellers, hunters like their prairie cousins, but relying on beaver, elk and moose rather than exclusively on the buffalo. Some of the Assiniboine in Saskatchewan and Montana speak of the Stoneys as the "lost tribe" of the Assiniboine (Kennedy 1972: 73). The Stoneys on the other hand claim that they have never been "lost" at all, they have been mountain and foothill people since time immemorial. Drawing on tribal tradition and oral history, Chief John Snow (1977: 2) assumes that the Stoneys' traditional hunting territory extended north to the Brazeau River - Jasper area, south a little past what is now the international border, east beyond the present-day city of Calgary and west into the Rockies beyond what was to become the British Columbia border.

This is suggested by historical records. Even if we disregard Henry Kelsey's encounters with "mountain poets" (Williams 1955: 107) on the Saskatchewan prairie as early as the 17th century, there is the evidence of Henday (1753-54) (MacGregor 1954: 164 f on "Asinepoets"), of Henry (1808) and many others (Laurie 1957/59: 19) to suggest, that prior to a dispersal of Plains Assiniboine by smallpox in 1780 Stoneys were occupying lands along the lower Battle River, the Athabasca, the Pembina, the North Saskatchewan, and in the deeper foothills.

They can be divided into two major groups: the Strong Woods of the Battle River, and the Swampy Grounds back in the foothills. These groups slightly differed in their way of life: The Strong Woods (remnants of whom today live at Wabamun Lake/Paul Band and Lac Ste Anne/Alexis Band) were partially adapted to the horse and buffalo culture of the plains and traded in horses with the Crees and later in fur and meat with the fur companies. The Swampy Grounds were almost strictly a forest people, owned only few horses and relied on their dogs for transport, hunted forest animals for food, and trapped beaver and other small fur animals. Like the Blackfoot, in its nomadic way of life the tribe never travelled as

9

a unit, but lived in several bands, usually breaking off into smaller extended-family groups when moving about. In winter the band came together in protected winter camp grounds. The entire tribe gathered only for ceremonial and other special occasions.

The Stoneys' first direct contact with Europeans occurred in the area near Rocky Mountain House around 1800, and they became suppliers of fresh meat, mainly deer and moose. This resulted in material changes in their life: Steel axes, knives and firearms replaced the traditional home-made tools and weapons; woven cloth was utilized besides skins. By the 1850s, the horse had almost completely replaced the dog as a means of transportation. By and large, however, the Stoneys' traditional life continued unchanged. As in the case of the Blackfoot, trade with the whites never became the basis of their economy. The Stoneys traded only for certain commodities and continued to support themselves by their own hunting. In the second half of the 19th century the tribe still occupied the whole area from the headwaters of the North Saskatchewan to the international border. Three main groups could be identified: In the south, along the foothills to the Crowsnest Pass, the Bearspaw band lived, adhering to a semi-plains way of life and being among the most warlike of the tribe. They frequently engaged in intertribal skirmishes, especially with the Blackfoot. North of them in the Bow River region were the Chiniki, who also often extended their hunting activities out onto the plains. The Goodstoney band occupied the northernmost part of the tribal territory, near Kootenay Plains and the North Saskatchewan River. They subsisted almost entirely as a woodland people. In spring and fall the partly plains-oriented bands used to move onto the plains to hunt buffalo. During the remainder of the year they travelled along the foothills, subsisting on elk, deer, moose and other forest animals. The three bands' respective winter camp grounds were the Highwood River area, the site of today's Morleyville and the Kootenay Plains.

We can conclude this chapter by stating, that at the close of the 1860s neither the native population's physical survival nor their cultural survival was threatened to any notable degree. There had been ravages by disease and alcohol among the Stoneys and Peigan as among the other northwestern tribes, but on the whole their culture had flourished, and their efficiency of environmental exploitation had increased. The relationship between the Indian and the European was based upon the co-operative exploitation of the fur resources of the region. During this period there existed the kind of reciprocity between the two races that is implied by the word "relationship", but with settlement the word "impact" more appropriately describes the effect of one culture on the other.

Chapter 3

Treaty Number Seven and early Reserve Days

The year 1870 witnessed the transfer of Rupert's Land and the Northwestern Territory from the Hudson's Bay Company to the Dominion of Canada, which led to the implementation of the federal government's Indian policy in this area, and threw open the land for settlement. This event transformed the western interior from a colony of exploitation, which made use of indigenous manpower into a colony of settlement, where the Indians became at best irrelevant, and at worst an obstacle to the purposes of the Europeans.

Governmental Indian policy in western Canada was an extension of methods that had developed in the eastern part of Canada during the previous century. Since the 1820s the necessity of securing the native tribes as military and commercial allies had declined, and the main goal now was to "civilize and settle" them. This was to be achieved by Christianity, education and agriculture, the holy trinity of British colonial policy on aborigines (Fisher 1977: 68). The major steps were alienation of Indian interest in land through treaties, their settling on inalienable reserves and exposing them to the influence of missions, schools and agricultural instructors, while a government department was charged with the management of Indian affairs. The roots of this policy go back to the Royal Proclamation of 1763: Both Crown title and aboriginal right in the soil were implied, while it was reserved to the Crown alone to acquire Indian land by extinguishing aboriginal title. The treaty concerned with the Stoneys and Peigan was the so-called Blackfoot Treaty, the seventh in a series of eleven post-confederation treaties (1) (the "numbered treaties"). It was signed at Blackfoot Crossing on September 22, 1877, between representatives of the Crown and the three tribes of the Blackfoot Confederation, the allied Sarcee, and the Stoneys. Subject of the treaty was the unsurrendered southwest portion of the territory (including about 80,000 square kilometres/ 30,888 square miles), located north of the international boundary line, east of the Rocky Mountains, south of the Red Deer River and west of the Cypress Hills. The main elements of Treaty Seven may be summarized as follows (see Copy of Treaty No. 7):

1) a relinquishment of the Indian right and title to the lands as outlined above

2) permission of the Indians' hunting and fishing throughout the ceded territory "subject to such regulations as may, from time to time, be made by the Government of the country, acting under the authority of Her Majesty and saving and excepting such Tracts as may be required or taken up from time to time for settlement, mining, trading or other purposes by Her Government of Canada; or by any of Her Majesty's subjects duly authorized therefor by the said Government".

3) assignment of reserves to the Indians, allowing one square mile for each family of five persons, or in that proportion for larger and smaller families "The Reserve of the Stony Band of Indians shall be in the vicinity of Morleyville."
"The Reserve of the Peigan Band of Indians shall be on the Old Man's River, near the foot of the Porcupine Hills, at a place called 'Crow's Creek'."

4) annuities of five dollars a head to each Indian, of fifteen dollars to each councillor or headman and of twenty five dollars to each chief. Issue of clothing to chiefs and headmen once in every three years. Donation of silver medals and British flags;

5) issue of agricultural implements and/or livestock to form the nuclei of herds to the Indians;

6) provision for the instruction of Indian children.

The North Peigan were represented by their Head Chief, Sitting on an Eagle Tail, and three minor chiefs. For the Stoney tribe, each band signed separately: Chief Kichipwot (Jacob Goodstoney), Chief Chiniquai (Chiniki) and Chief Bearspaw, each chief with his own councillors. These three chiefs were considered head chiefs for the entire Stoney tribe by the commissioners.

The Stoneys' participation in Treaty Seven, however, is not without controversy. One wonders, why the Stoneys were invited to sign Treaty Seven rather than an adhesion to Treaty Six or the subsequent Treaty Eight. The above outline of the area to be covered by Treaty Seven shows that it includes only that portion of the Stoneys' territory which lies south of the Red Deer River, namely the area

---

1) For detailed information on the treaty itself see Copy of Treaty and Supplementary Treaty No. 7, Made 22nd Sept., and 4th Dec., 1877, between Her Majesty the Queen and the Blackfeet and Other Indian Tribes, at the Blackfoot Crossing of Bow River and Fort MacLeod, reprinted by Queen's Printer, Ottawa, 1966; and for information about discussion and events at the actual time of the signing, see Alexander Morris, 1880, The Treaties of Canada with the Indians, Toronto: Willing & Williamson. The different interpretations of the treaties by native people and whites will be discussed in Chapter 4 of this study.

around Morleyville, while the Bighorn-Kootenay Plains region lies north of the boundary line (Fig. 3). The council order appointing the treaty commission (Copy of Treaty No. 7: 2) did not even mention a negotiation with the Stoney tribe as an

Figure 3: The Location of the Kootenay Plains and the Treaty Areas

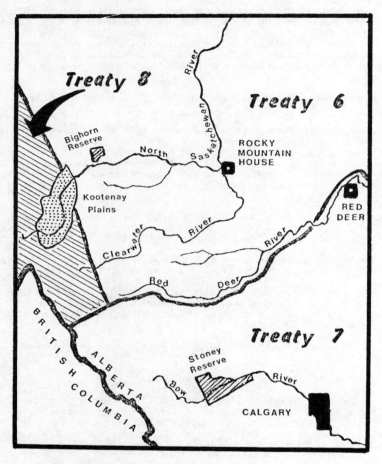

Source: Adapted from Snow (1977), p. 38

explicit goal: "That the Territory to be included in the proposed Treaty is occupied by the Blackfeet, Crees, Sarcees and Peigan ..." And the same strange failure to mention them is obvious in most official reports and correspondence concerning this treaty (Morris 1880: 245-275). John McDougall - the Wesleyan missionary who had established a permanent mission among the Stoneys in 1873, and who was instrumental in preparing Treaty Seven -, when questioned in 1876 by the Dominion Government, which date and location would be most convenient to negotiate a treaty with the Stoneys even suggested their adhesion to Treaty Six, which had already been signed (Alexander Morris Papers, cited in Snow, p. 34), since the larger part of their territory came under the purview of this treaty. Yet, when coming to Blackfoot Crossing to conclude Treaty Seven, Lieutenant Governor Laird apparently assumed, that the entire Stoney tribe was present to sign the new treaty, as possibly he had been given the impression, that all the bands were living at Morleyville. John McDougall, adviser and interpreter in the promotion of this treaty, never questioned this decision, and no further mention of the northern Stoney territory was made. Not only Snow (1977: 35), but also Dempsey (1978 a: 45) and Larner (1976: 45) suggest that it must have been very convenient for the missionary to have the entire tribe concentrated on one single reserve at Morleyville, where mission and agricultural estate were located. On the other hand, when signing the treaty, and relying on verbal assurances that they would be given reserves in their traditional hunting grounds, Chief Kichipwot expected to receive a similar reserve in the Bigborn-Kootenay Plains area for his people, and Chief Bearspaw thought he would be allocated land for his band south of Morley. Moreover, there is ample evidence that various bands residing permanently on the Kootenay Plains and living along the foothills south of Morley were not present at the treaty negotiations. It is doubtful whether the three tribal leaders, regarded as head chiefs by the commissioners were authorized to make decisions on their behalf.

After the treaty the Indians were convinced that they would be allowed to continue their traditional hunting way of life, especially as the buffalo, until the following year, 1878, were still present in comparatively large numbers (Roe 1934: 16). In his account on the negotiations Lieutenant Governor Laird (Morris 1880: 262) presumes that the buffalo would last for ten more years, and that by this time the Indians would be able to subsist on their herds of domestic cattle. The Stoneys were reportedly the only tribe to ask for seed and agricultural implements instead, a request which Snow (1977: 33) attributes to John McDougall's influence. The missionary wished to establish a sedentary community adjacent to the mission. Although he had converted a small segment of the tribe to an agrarian lifestyle, the Stoneys did not adopt agriculture as their main livelihood. Not only were the Stoneys a hunting people with all those cultural and socio-economic characteristics that render a rapid transformation impossible, but also the physical endowment of the reserve at Morleyville was to prove completely unsuited for crop-raising.

Although the location of the reserves was decided on during the treaty negotiations, their actual survey was not to take place until a few years later, in 1879, the year the buffalo disappeared on the Canadian side of the border. This delay was due mainly to a lack of surveyors (McQuillan 1980: 384). Surveying crews were busy preparing the land for white settlers who were expected to flood to the "fertile belt", since at that time one anticipated the transcontinental railroad to pass through the parkland belt. Meanwhile those Indians who did not follow the dwindling buffalo herds across the border, had to subsist on rabbits, gophers and mice.

In 1879 A.P. Patrick, District Land Surveyor, arrived at Morleyville to survey the Stoney reserve. Contrary to the Indians' assumption mentioned above, there was no further discussion as to location and number of the reserve(s). Patrick had come to survey only land surrounding the Methodist mission, and for just one reserve. Another significant feature was the fact, that only Chief Chiniki was present at Morley, when the survey was conducted, while Chief Bearspaw (of the southern band) and Chief Kichipwot (of the northern section of the tribe) were in their respective territories on hunting expeditions. Nobody tried to notify them. Meanwhile, Chiniki, chief of the smallest band, and himself under the impression that he was receiving land only for his band, dealt with the surveyor, aided by McDougall as translator. Patrick in turn considered Chiniki as spokesman for the entire tribe, and the same was to happen again eight years later, when J.C. Nelson resurveyed the reserve. The report on the second survey states explicitly that "the land is not adapted for farming purposes, and a greater part of it is only fit for grazing" (Indian Affairs 1889, Indian Reserve Plans, p. 101).

Yet the boundaries and location of the reserve were not to be disputed for some time, as all tribes in 1880 were faced by a major crisis: the disappearance of the buffalo. It occurred much sooner than even the Europeans had anticipated, and meant disaster for those tribes exclusively dependent on these great beasts. The Peigan and other neighbouring tribes had no choice other than going to their reserves (only there rations were issued) or starving. Even though the government did make efforts to provide rations, the 1880s witnessed gruelling scenes of starvation (Roe 1934: 20 f). The Stoneys were far less severely affected by the extermination of the buffalo. Though they always had killed buffalo their hunting economy was more diversified than it was with the plains tribes, and they continued to subsist on moose, elk, deer, wild sheep and goats, although it now required a more extensive and far-ranging hunt to support themselves. The rations issued by the Indian agent were merely used to provide for the elderly and sick, who could not go out on the hunt. The Morley Reserve took on the function of a base-camp for more and more members of the tribe (Snow 1977: 43). A pattern emerged in which most of the people wintered at Morleyville or other traditional sites and returned each summer to their respective hunting grounds to carry on their traditional life style. Yet several families lived permanently on the Kootenay Plains, and others south of the Morley Reserve. Mainly due to lack of funds the government did not interfere with the Stoneys' persistence in their old ways. They were only too glad to see at least one tribe capable of providing for itself, as agriculture had, meanwhile, proven a complete failure. In 1884 rations were cut off from the tribe except for the infirm and in emergencies (Dempsey 1978: 47).

Yet this comparatively happy situation was not going to last. In the mid-eighties game suddenly became scarce, and the hunters had to venture farther and farther into the mountains to shoot anything at all. They too, came to rely increasingly on rations, when again issued to the whole tribe. The primary cause for this new development was the completion of the Canadian Pacific Railway in 1885 and the rapid influx of white settlers (Laurie 1957-59: 1). Ranchers and farmers came, and at the same time private enterprise began exploiting the coal, copper and timber along the railway line. Moreover, "visiting sportsmen" came, killing off the Indians' food supply. The scarcity of game induced the Stoneys to cross the Alberta-Montana border (still within their traditional hunting grounds) and to make frequent excursions into British Columbia; the latter gave rise to conflicts with the Kutenai and Shuswap, living along the Columbia River. An agreement was reached in 1892, establishing the Continental Divide as boundary between the two tribal hunting territories (Laurie Papers, pp. 3-5). A further reduction of the Stoneys' hunting grounds had occurred with the creation of the Banff National Park in 1887, then Rocky Mountain Park.

From 1885 onwards there had been an increasing public pressure on the government to keep the Stoneys on their reserve and away from their hunting grounds. Ironically, one reason given for this was that the Indians were responsible for the diminution in wildlife. In the first place, however, this trend was part of a general great outcry against Indian people after the second Riel rebellion in 1885, even though neither the Peigan nor the Stoneys had taken up arms against the Canadian government. Complying with the public request for "protection", the Indian Affairs Branch enforced a pass-system to control the natives' movements and to confine them within the boundaries of their reserves (contrary to their treaty right of hunting in unoccupied crown land). While this regulation was apparently not really enforced on Stoney hunting activities (Snow 1977: 53) for several years, the constantly deteriorating public view of Indians led in 1893 to what was in Indian eyes the first outright breaking of the treaty: The Indian Affairs Branch embarked upon a policy of curtailing the Indians' hunting by subjecting Treaty Indians to the general game laws of the Northwest Territories. Simultaneously a cut-back in rations occurred. In 1895 Indian-White relations deteriorated to their lowest level since the Riel insurrection.

A direct outcome of this deteriorated situation was Moosekiller's (Peter Wesley) move out of the Morley Reserve onto the Kootenay Plains in 1894: He led approximately 100 members (one-third) of the Goodstoney Band back to their ancestral territory in the north, along the banks of the North Saskatchewan River. His decision to defy government policy was the prelude to the "Kootenay Plains Land Question", which was to become a "touchstone" of Canadian Indian policy in the twentieth century (see Chapter 5.2.1.1). As will be remembered the larger northern section of the Stoney tribal territory was not covered by Treaty Seven nor was there an adhesion to Treaty Six which did not include it either. This fact is rather surprising, since the valley of the upper North Saskatchewan River was widely thought of as potentially rich in both coal and gold by the time these two treaties were signed. Moreover, it was universally regarded as the easiest route over the mountains to British Columbia. This omission was only discovered when Treaty Eight was signed in 1899, mainly with the Cree, Beaver and Chipewyan. It focussed on northern Alberta and the North West Territories south of the Great Slave Lake, but incorporated the strip of land bordering the Great Divide north of the Red Deer River (Fig. 3). Yet the Stoneys of the Bighorn-Kootenay Plains were not invited to participate in the Treaty Eight settlement.

The question of the reserve boundaries did not become overt as long as they were not enforced as such (during the early 1880s), but as early as 1889, five years before Moosekiller's exodus, the tribal council at Morleyville petitioned the Indian Affairs Branch to enlarge the reserve by means of an extension to the existing reserve on the north side of the Bow River. The main reason was that - farming being well-nigh impossible and game being scarce on the reserve - additional pasturage and hay lands were required for ranching, apparently the only realistic means of self-support on the reserve. At first this request was immediately turned down, then met with alternative suggestions to extend the southern and western boundaries. The twenty-five years following the Stoneys' application were characterized by tentative considerations of the original proposal, conflicts between the Indian Affairs Branch and the Department of the Interior, title searches conducted by the latter, new rejections and a temporary short-term land lease of a small section to provide timber for the band. It was not before 1914 that some Crown lands were transferred to the reserve in response to the population increase; 5,157 hectar (12,743 acres) north of Morley by Rabbit Lake (Saller Lake), Reserve 142 B.

By the turn of the century the Stoneys had not undergone any abrupt change in their general pattern of earning a livelihood. But nevertheless they had become thoroughly disillusioned with the federal government. The surveying of the reserve, the influx of a large number of white settlers, the building of the Canadian Pacific Railway right through the reserve (The Stoneys who were not even consulted had to turn over hundreds of acres of valuable grazing land including mineral rights), the establishment of National Parks and the attempts to confine them to their reserve by means of the pass-system, had put the Stoneys under considerable pressure. Crop-raising had proven a failure due to frost and inadequate soil, but the Stoneys' interest in cattle was gradually increasing, as the reserve offered good grazing. Another activity was the cutting of timber, which was purchased by Indian Affairs to be utilized on the wood-deficient plains-reserves.

The Peigan faced a much more drastic change when they first settled on their reserve in spring 1880. The reserve was not surveyed before 1882. They were the first of the three Blackfoot tribes to accept the sedentary lifestyle as a group. The Peigan were anxious to find a new source of livelihood and willingly turned to the soil. Crops of potatoes, turnips, oats and barley were planted, and by the end of the year they had more than a hundred acres under crop and built fifty houses, using timber from their Timber Limit (surveyed in 1888) in the nearby Porcupine Hills. Their small farms were mostly in the river bottom of the Oldman River. As part of the treaty obligations the Peigan had also received their cattle, but initially these animals were kept together with the government herd on the north end of the reserve, mainly as a source of beef for rations. Farming was given top priority, and the initial results were so encouraging that as early as 1881 the Inspector of Agencies said, "These Indians are very well to do and will, in my opinion, be the first of the Southern Plains Indians to become selfsupporting" (Indian Affairs Annual Report 1881: 178). Rations were reduced; the Indians were issued permits to sell their surplus produce of potatoes, and in 1883 even supplied the Blackfoot, Sarcee and Stoney Reserves with seed. By 1885 they produced more potatoes than they could consume and sell, and, not surprisingly, they became very reluctant to increase the size of their small farms. But then the few good crop years came to an end.

In 1886 a severe drought reduced the potatoes to the size of marbles, and the grain was cut for fodder. Over the next fifteen years one crop failure followed another. Although the failure of the experiment was recognized in the early 1890s, government policy dictated that the Indians be encouraged to farm, so the work went on. At the same time they were hemmed in by regulations and restrictions wherever they turned. In order to keep them occupied and to further the process of individualization and subdivision of reserve land (both of which was meant to prepare them for enfranchisement), the Peigan were discouraged from communal farming operations (Only hay and wood lands were held in common) and from the use of labor saving equipment (Indian Affairs Annual Report 1889: 163 ff). Only in 1898 did the government finally admit its mistake and defeat. "Climatic conditions of wind, drought and frost prohibit successful farming on this reserve," stated Agent Wilson (ibid.), and he goes on:

> For about fifteen years a large outlay has been annually made in labour and seed while fruitlessly attempting to grow grain here. While the preparation of the ground was wholesome - though discouraging - occupation for the Indians, the seed grain was literally thrown away, and it is, therefore, the intention of the agency to make no further efforts in that direction but to concentrate all possible attention to cattle-raising, for which the reserve and its inhabitants are better suited.

In the meantime the herd of cattle had continued to grow, and in the later 1880s many of the animals had been turned over to individual owners. In 1888 a system of close herding was adopted, rather than allowing them to range at large, as was common practice on white ranches. This was done in order to save the government "the expense of placing men on the spring and fall round-ups to look after the Indians' interests, while the Indians themselves, even if they knew the work required of them, and their horses could do their part, are not wanted by cattle men among wild cattle at the round-ups for various reasons" (Indian Affairs Annual Report 1888: 95). By 1890 the Peigans' cattle numbered 141 head, and each year they were permitted to sell a few steers. Only five years later there were 868 head of cattle, partly due to the Indians trading many of their ponies for cattle. They also tried to upgrade their horses, as most of the Indian ponies were too small to perform satisfactory fieldwork. The successful introduction of livestock raising had other favourable effects. Now there was work for other Indians as herders, to cut and sell hay, and to cut and haul rail and posts for fences. Many individuals were engaged in freighting (using their own horses), selling ponies (especially during the Klondike goldrush, 1898), selling horse tack, rawhide ropes, beadwork, and butchering, scouting or breaking horses. In 1900 the Peigan received around 2,100 dollars as compensation for the right of way of the Crowsnest Railway across the reserve; they invested this money in a sawmill, located on the Timber Limit in the Porcupine Hills. As the individual Indians did their logging on shares with the mill, which was tribal property, a large quantity of lumber went to the working Indians, and the rest was sold off the reserve to offset mill operating expense.

During the 1880s and 1890s the Peigan suffered from many of the white man's diseases, particularly scrofula and tuberculosis. As a result, the mortality rate was high, and the tribe experienced a steady decline in population. Since their earliest days on the reserve (except for two years, 1885-1887) the Peigan had had their resident missionary, and by the turn of the century there were both Anglican and Roman Catholic boarding schools and churches. Both, however, did not meet with much success. As far as economic development goes, there were successful individuals, hailed as examples by the Indian Agent; but there were also scores of others dispirited and demoralized by life on the reserve, who subsisted on the meagre rations. There is much evidence in the Indian Affairs Annual Reports that rations in the 1890s were being cut back as a conscious policy of forcing Indians to become self-supporting.

By 1900 the reserve system was being questioned as a means of assimilation (1), and consequently the next years were to bring massive assaults on the Indian landbase. Since its inception in 1876 constant amendments had been made to the Indian Act to suit the government's newly arising goals. Yielding to political pressure - after an increase in the stream of migrants to the newly established prairie provinces of Alberta and Saskatchewan - the government revised the Indian Act in 1907, making it simpler and more attractive for bands to surrender their reserves. As the deputy superintendent stated (Indian Affairs Annual Report 1908: xxxv):

> So long as no particular harm nor inconvenience accrued from the Indians' holding vacant lands out of proportion to their requirements ... the department firmly opposed any attempt to induce them to divest themselves of any part of their reserves. Conditions, however, have changed and it is now recognized that where Indians are holding tracts of farming or timber lands beyond their possible requirements and by so doing seriously impeding the growth of settlement, ... it is in the beste interest of all concerned to encourage such sales.

The Peigan were disinclined to surrender any of their land for sale, but in 1909 the government forced a vote regarding the sale of the northwest corner of the reserve, and claimed it was approved. A chief, Big Swan, immediately prepared an affidavit claiming that the vote was fraudulent, but he was ignored, and by the end of the year 9,040 hectar (22,338 acres) of Indian land were surrendered, and more than half of it sold immediately. The land-poor Stoneys, on the other hand, were in a situation where they required more reserve land, rather than giving up what they had.

In 1918 the Indian Act was amended once more, this time in order to empower the department to lease reserve land without a previous surrender, even if the band council actively opposed such action "... through some delusion, misapprehension or hostility ..." (Indian Affairs Annual Report 1918: 20). This move was taken as part of the Greater Production campaign. In this case the Peigan were somewhat less affected than the Blood and Blackfoot, both of whom had to accommodate government Greater Production Farms on their reserves. The Peigan only leased land to white individuals.

By this time ranching was still the main source of income on the Peigan Reserve, but the development of new varieties of grain, better adapted to the climatic and soil conditions of the area, brought a reintroduction of farming on a small scale. For this purpose a suitable area, conveniently close to the railway, was subdivided into 65 hectar (160 acres) plots for the Indian farmers. In 1910 there were again ten Peigan farmers, compared to eighty-two individuals engaged in stockraising, but the formers' number was on the increase. The next blow though was soon to come. The period after the First World War witnessed a massive shift towards mechanization. As long as farming had remained relatively simple, the Indians were able to compete with non-Indian farmers. But when the conversion was made from the small scale horse-and-plough style of farming to larger acreages, with mechanized equipment, bank loans, and a knowledge of modern business techniques, the average Indian had neither the education nor the cultural conditioning to compete, and he slipped farther and farther behind his white neighbours. Until things picked up slightly after the second World War the Peigan neither regressed nor progressed.

While the Stoneys may have started their reserve years with a greater degree of self-sufficiency than the surrounding tribes, this margin was lost during the

---

1) For a detailed outline of the changes in focus of Canadian Indian policy see Tobias, J.L., 1976, Protection, Civilization, Assimilation: An Outline History of Canada's Indian Policy. <u>The Western Canadian Journal of Anthropology</u> 6, No, pp. 13-30.

passing years as hunting and travelling restrictions made it impossible for the people to live off the land. Many Stoneys worked off the reserve after the turn of the century; others continued to raise cattle and horses, to deliver logs to a sawmill, to cut firewood, posts and rails, and to haul wood to Kananaskis lime kilns and Exshaw. In 1910 there were also 10 farmers besides 65 ranchers.

The Stoneys continued to be plagued by their land shortage, but yet there were further inroads. In 1914 the Seebe dam was built, and the Calgary Power Company acquired reserve land upon which to locate their facilities. During the late 1920s the Ghost Dam was constructed, and the resulting reservoir flooded a portion of the reserve. Transmission line rights-of-way through the Stoney Reserve were given to Calgary Power; these served to break up the reserve and to reduce the amount of usable land. As usual, Chiefs and Council were only notified after the deal was settled, and were left under the impression that the land was only being leased, not sold (Getty 1974: 106). As was the case with the Canadian Pacific Railway, the mineral rights were turned over to Calgary Power, too. Furthermore, there were no provisions made to guarantee the Stoney people either the use of water in the dam or access to the lake edge. When the Banff Highway was constructed through the reserve (Highway 1A), the Stoneys were not compensated at all (1). By 1929 the discovery of natural oil and gas in commercial quantities in the Turner Valley had resulted in considerable attention being focused on some of the reserves, as they seemed to be located within the same oil belt which runs from northern Montana up through the Turner Valley district. Therefore a number of leases were issued by the Department of Indian Affairs on the Stoney Reserve.

Moosekiller and his Goodstoney followers were not the only ones to split from the group residing at Morley. Similarly, a number of Bearspaw's people had left the reserve in 1918 to escape the ravages of an influenza epidemic; they went to settle permanently in their traditional hunting territory to the south, along the Highwood and Pekisko Rivers. Their requests for a reserve in this area were disregarded by the government, as previous requests had been. During the next twenty-five years they eked out an existence, occasionally working for nearby ranchers (Laurie 1957-59: 39) and supplementing their income by hunting in the foothills and mountains. Yet, in the early 1940s their plight was so pitiful that the government finally yielded: In 1946 a 2,024 hectar (5,000 acres) ranch on the Highwood River was bought and converted into the Eden Valley Reserve. Later it was enlarged by a lease of provincial land.

In 1945 the Stoneys were given the chance to make another substantial addition to their reserve, though it was to be a costly undertaking for the tribe. To enable the Stoneys to pay for the new land the government loaned them a sum of $ 500,000 for an indefinite period at three per cent interest per year. This interest would be collected from the fees paid to the tribe by Calgary Power. The loan was used to purchase the Ralph C. Coppock "Merino" Ranch near Cochrane and the Arthur Crawford Ranch adjoining the Morley Reserve. However, instead of utilizing the land to provide much needed pasture and hay land for the cattle already on the reserve, the Indian Affairs department decided to develop a band herd on the new ranch in order to increase band funds. There was no attempt to use the ranch as a training project or to provide any other positive effect on the community. Many band members were trying hard to expand their livestock operations into viable economic units but ended up having to sell cattle in order to buy enough feed to bring the remainder through the winter. A few severe winters in the 1950s killed off many of the cattle, and most people just gave up and sold the remaining animals. Subsequently, more and more land was leased to neighbouring ranchers. Hay fields were retained by the band so that members could harvest winter feed for their horses.

---

1) In the case of the Trans-Canada Highway though, in 1961, the Department of Indian Affairs initiated direct negotiations between the Band Council and the Provincial Government. In exchange for the land given up for the highway, the Stoneys received additional land adjacent to the northern boundary of the Morley Reserve.

During the 1950s and 1960s there was some improvement in the Alberta Indians' situation. Health services improved and tuberculosis was virtually eliminated. Educational facilities were upgraded, and the government changed its policy of discouraging education beyond the age of sixteen and gradually phased out the church-operated residential schools. But where development of the reserves is concerned, and a say of the band members in their own affairs, not much was accomplished. The Department of Indian Affairs was still in absolute control of every aspect of reserve life. On the Stoney Reserve the natural gas wells had proven productive, and, therefore, more funds became available. They were used to develop roads, wells and other general services. But there was no attempt to help the people to help themselves, they were given no chance to take advantage of their own resource base. The store, the gas station, the YMCA-camp, the sawmill and the ranching enterprises within the reserve were all owned and operated by white people on a lease base. Only the sawmill provided employment to band members, but they were only hired to cut logs.

On the Peigan Reserve, at that time, the situation is best described by the word "stagnation". Horses and cattle were still being kept, but a huge amount of grazing land and virtually all arable land was leased out to white farmers and ranchers, without the band council receiving the returns it was entitled to. The band's sawmill had closed down, but intermittent logging was still carried out on the Timber Limit in the 1960s.

In the 1960s reserves throughout Canada started pressing for more control of their own affairs. Band councils wanted to develop their own programs and administer their own funds. In 1966 the federal government finally yielded to the pressure and announced its program of local reserve self-government. The Peigan and the Stoneys were among the first in Alberta to accept the challenge of assuming administration of their own reserves.

Chapter 4

Aspirations for the Future (1)

The reserves functioning under the system of local self-government are by no means autonomous. They are still subject to the Indian Act; they are still under the final control of the Indian Affairs department, and they are subject to certain federal and provincial laws and regulations. But within these boundaries the Band Chiefs and Councils now have a certain degree of freedom to identify and pursue the directions and goals of reserve development. For the first time people have the opportunity to exert some influence over the changes occurring in their life.

When we look at the aspirations or goals of the Stoneys, Peigan and other treaty-Indians, there are certain main themes that keep confronting us. Prominent among these are the Indian people's relationship with the dominant society, their status with regard to this society, and the development of their reserves as ethnic homelands. It goes without saying that these issues are inseparately interrelated.

Even today native people whose forefathers signed treaties with representatives of the British Crown view their relationship with the wider society and its government in terms of their treaties. At the same time, government and Indian leaders tend to operate within two completely different systems of knowledge and perceptions of reality regarding basic "treaty rights" issues (Price 1979: XI). When Treaty

---

(1) As a non-Indian I do not pretend to speak on this subject with any authority; but after associating with Indian organizations as well as with individuals - both politicians and non-politicians - I feel capable of at least presenting some ideas.

Seven was signed in 1877 the government of that day did not regard treaties as anything like a social contract in which different ways of life were accommodated within mutually acceptable limits. Treaties were a means of land surrender, once and for all, and thus were more important for what Indians gave up than for the concessions given to Indians. There is no recorded evidence, however, that the commissioners attempted at the treaty negotiations to explain what they meant by a surrender. Reference to settlers and other newcomers was usually made in connection with the idea of keeping the peace, not molesting these people and allowing them to share the land. Given their cultural attitude towards use and ownership, this concept would have been familiar to the Indians of the time. This lack of emphasis in the negotiations on the surrender by the Indians of their territory is in sharp contrast to the prominence and explicit detail of the surrender clauses of the treaty texts (Taylor 1979: 41). Interviews conducted with elders on the Treaty Seven Reserves (under the Stoney Cultural Education Program and as part of the Treaty and Aboriginal Rights Research of the Indian Association of Alberta), whose parents were present at the negotiations, show unanimous consent on the fact, that Treaty Seven was understood as a peace treaty. In contrast to Treaty Six, where the interviewed agree that surface rights (not mineral rights) had been surrendered, not one elder in the Treaty Seven area mentioned that the treaty had anything to do with giving up land or even sharing it with white people. Therefore, there is general agreement among Alberta's Indians that at least they should receive more benefits from mineral wealth since it comes from land they had occupied, not to mention hunting and trapping privileges.

But there is not only disagreement between the parties about what was given up by the Indian people; there is just as much dissension about what they can expect in return. First there is the problem of "outside promises": The making of the treaties took the form of verbal discussion between the Commissioners and the Indians. The written texts, with their very legalistic construction, were prepared later by government lawyers. Therefore, as the "Red Paper" (Indian Chiefs of Alberta 1970: 26) states, the formal written treaties (small t) are insufficient as reports of the Treaties (large T), of the verbal promises exchanged by Indians and Whites.

Even more contentious is the discrepancy between the precise wording of the written treaty on the one hand, and the "spirit" of the treaty on the other hand. The Modern Canadian Dictionary defines spirit as the "true intent or meaning as opposed to outward formal observance: the spirit of the law" (Price 1979: XIII). Thus the policy interpretations applied to the treaties have assumed a moral rather than a legal character. "Treaties that run forever must have room for the changes in the conditions of life," says the Red Paper (p. 8). Applying this interpretation, the provision of teachers by the federal government was a commitment to provide Indian children the educational opportunity equal to their white neighbours. Machinery and livestock symbolized a lasting commitment to economic development. Especially in the case of economic development - it is significant that the promise of agricultural aid was only added in the numbered treaties at the insistence of the Indians (Taylor 1979: 3-7) - Indian leaders now emphasize that it is "a treaty right, not merely a matter of government policy" (Indian Association of Alberta 1977: 7). The government on the other hand tends to follow its legal obligations according to the strict written terms of the treaties, an approach that results in an overall sense of betrayal on the part of the treaty Indians. Moreover, although the treaties were ratified, they were never legislated to carry the force of law. Indians now demand an incorporation of the treaties in updated terms in an amendment to the Canadian Constitution.

An event that involuntarily resulted in Indians becoming very vocal in the articulation of their goals was the release of the federal government's so-called "White Paper" (Statement of the Government of Canada on Indian Policy) in 1969 (1).

---

1) For the events surrounding the federal government's formulation of the White Paper, see Weaver, S.M., 1981, <u>Making Canadian Indian Policy. The Hidden Agenda 1968-1970</u>, Toronto: University of Toronto Press.

The then new Liberal government adopted a new approach to Indian affairs that emphasized individual equality and de-emphasized collective ethnic survival. Indians as individuals were to be helped at the expense of Indians as a people (Ponting and Gibbins 1980: 26). More specifically the White Paper proposed that the legislative and constitutional bases for discrimination be removed; the Indian Act was to be repealed. Indians were to receive the same services as other Canadians, and these were to be delivered through the same channels and from the same government agencies as serviced other citizens. The unique federal government responsibility for Indians was to end. The Indian Affairs Program with in the Department of Indian Affairs and Northern Development was to be abolished. Moreover, the control of Indian lands should be transferred to the Indian people; land would no longer be held in trust for Indians by the Crown. The White Paper also recognized that any lawful obligations (in the narrowest sense of the word) that the government had incurred through the signing of the treaties must be recognized. Finally it advocated selective aid to those bands economically farthest behind rather than universal aid programs, and it called for a "positive recognition by everyone of the unique contribution of Indian culture to Canadian life" (Government of Canada 1969: 6). Altogether the White Paper reflected the American civil rights movement more clearly than the reality of Canadian Indian conditions. As Weaver (1981: 7 f and 131) points out, it was very much a response to values within the policy-making arena of the national government, and was designed more to protect the government from external criticism than to meet the aspirations of Canadian Indians as these were perceived by Indians themselves. The White Paper departed very significantly from the Hawthorn Report (see Chapter 1) which had been generally well-received by the Indian community. Whereas the White Paper proclaimed an undisguised assimilation policy the Hawthorn Report called for the retention of Indians as a unique ethnic group and even went as far as recommending that they be given the status of "citizen plus" with certain additional rights as charter members of the Canadian community (Hawthorn 1966 Part 1: 13). The Hawthorn Report became a focal reference point for Indian opposition, and the concept of "citizen plus" became title and cornerstone of the "Red Paper", the Alberta Indians' response to and violent rebuttal of the White Paper. The Indian Chiefs of Alberta argue that discrimination in fact may exist even when discrimination in law has been abolished, and that equality in fact may even necessitate the special legal protection of minority rights (and hence the recognition of Indian status). The Red Paper demands that the Indian Act must be reviewed and amended to provide a legal basis for tribal government, but not repealed. The treaties should be incorporated in updated terms in an amendment to the Canadian Constitution, and the special relationship with the federal government be maintained (including the provision of a full-time Minister of Indian Affairs). As to "Indian Control of Indian Lands", the Alberta Indians express their opposition to any system of allotment that would give individuals ownership with rights to sell, and, in addition, would subject the land to provincial taxation. They insist that the Indian Act could be changed to give Indians control of lands without changing the fact that the title is held in trust. "It must be held forever in trust of the Crown because, as we say, 'The true owners of the land are not yet born'" (Indian Chiefs of Alberta 1970: 10).

What the retention of group identity really means to Indian people, is nowhere better expressed than by George Manuel: "Remaining Indian means that Indian people gain control of the economic and social development of our communities, within a framework of legal and constitutional guarantees for our land and our institutions" (Manuel and Posluns 1974: 221 f). The evolution of Canadian Indian policy shows quite clearly that Indians as a collectivity as well as their reserves were (and are) regarded as a transitory feature of Canadian society. Reserves were not considered lands reserved for Indian people for their homelands but as lands granted by the government to be used as schools for civilization and to be done away with once this purpose had been fulfilled. On the other hand there can be no doubt that Indians still promote the idea of the reserve as an ethnic homeland. This is shown by the continued residence of the majority of western Indians on their reserves - with the Stoneys and Peigan the percentage living off-reserve is in fact negligible - and the retention of close ties to their home community by most of the urban migrants; it is also evident from the endeavour of Indian politicians on all levels. At the same time the retention of Indian homelands does neither imply the conservation of a museum culture nor the clinging to economically bankrupt refuges. Indian people want economic viability, but they want it on their own terms and in their own style: "Economic well-being does not necessarily mean a high standard of living or great wealth, but rather freedom from want achieved through meaningful activity. It means having available and being able to choose from the widest possible range of options respecting lifestyle" (National Indian Brotherhood 1977: 83). As the Red Paper says, "It is important that everyone recognize that giving up our Indian identity is not necessary for economic development" (Indian Chiefs of Alberta 1970: 15). There are many arguments by non-Indians against the "doctrine of cultural relativism" as Davis (1968: 228) puts it, which he defines as an attitude that sees all cultures as "equally valuable and equally deserving of respect". And he goes on: "Perhaps all cultures are equally valuable in some special sense or other. They may even merit respect. But they are not equally viable. For all practical purposes a uniquely Indian way of life in Canada is already as dead as an Egyptian mummy" (ibid.). A statement like this contains the unspoken assumption that Indian culture is entirely static. But as the previous chapters have already shown, Indians can adapt and adjust without loss of their identity and self-awareness as Indian people. Historian Palmer Patterson (1972: 28 f) states

> ... that Western civilization has changed considerably since 1500, but is still thought of as Western civilization. This is due in part at least to the acceptance of the notion that Western civilization is always dynamic, and being so, change is built into the definition. Indian culture, being a priori static, cannot, by the alternative definition, adapt. Of course the overwhelming evidence is to the contrary. Indian cultures have changed greatly in the last four hundred years and have kept their identity.

While it may be true that Indian cultures originally evolved within now-abandoned economies, and values that have been retained do not comport with the economic practices of the white civilization, it does not mean that assimilation is the only road to economic survival. Indians are very well aware of the less desirable aspects of our civilization such as social desintegration and environmental abuse, and while they have developed a taste for many material items of Euro-Canadian culture they have little inclination to follow suit entirely. Socio-economic development of their own making is seen as a means to satisfy new consumer tastes and to retain of their culture what seems desirable to them. Socio-economic development is broadly defined by Alberta Indian leaders as "people development in conjunction with economic development" (Eugene Steinhauer and Joe Dion cited by Price and Marshall, 1979: 7); this is different from mere natural resource development under profit maximizing principles, as it went on under Department of Indian Affairs Management before the onset of self-government. The Stoney Band Council sees economic development within the reserve as having four main functions: to provide permament jobs for band members; to create opportunities for band members to develop specific skills and general knowledge; to improve the general standard of living and services available to band members; and to increase band revenue money. Quite similarly, the Peigan expect economic development to offer real alternatives to the dependency on Social Assistance and make-work programs; to provide training facilities; and to promote self-sufficiency and thereby create an atmosphere of self-esteem and pride. In their emphasis on human development and humane economic development that takes into account pre-existing socio-cultural features, the Stoneys and the Peigan are faced by a host of problems not all of which have been resolved yet. Their solution can only come from within the community. The subsequent chapters will attempt to show how two reserves are being turned into tribal homelands.

Chapter 5

The Land-based Economy

5.1 The physical-geographical Conditions

5.1.1 Topography

The three Stoney Reserves - the Morley Reserve including Rabbit Lake, Eden Valley and Bighorn - are all located in the foothills of the Rocky Mountains. On the Morley Reserve the elevation varies from 1,890 metres (6,200 feet) above sea level in the mountains in the northwest portion of the reserve to 1,190 metres (3,904 feet) above sea level at the Ghost Reservoir on the Bow River. With the exception of Morley Flats, a flat, gravelly plain east of the Kananaskis and Bow River confluence, the general topography of the reserve is rolling. The Rabbit Lake Reserve has a considerably more rugged terrain than Morley proper. Its main features are two northwesterly-oriented valleys, eroded in soft shales and separated by sandstone ridges. The only area of relatively flat land in this part of the reserve is the western valley surrounding Rabbit Lake. The Eden Valley Reserve lands rise in two-level terraces from the east bank of the Highwood River, the whole area sloping gently to the northwest. The Hughes Ranch has gently rolling terrain. The Bighorn Reserve is similar to Rabbit Lake in terrain. In its more level parts, near the confluence of the North Saskatchewan and Bighorn River, it contains large deposits of glacio-fluvial gravels over much of its width.

The main reserve of the Peigan is situated on the Oldman River near the foot of the Porcupine Hills. Its topography is rolling and varies in hight from 1,344 metres (4,409 feet) above sea level in the spurs of the Porcupine Hills in the northwest corner of the reserve to 975 metres (3,199 feet) at the river bottom. The Oldman River meanders through the reserve from southwest to northeast, the adjacent terrain being intensely gullied for short distances back of the edges of the valley. The land adjacent to the Oldman consists of lacustrine and alluvial clays, silts and fine sands, followed by preglacial gravels and sands over bedrock. The valley floor is underlain by channel and floodplain deposits. The Peigan Timber Limit is part of the Porcupine Hills. Maximum elevation is just over 1,754 metres (5,755 feet). Squaw Butte, a prominent landmark of the area, measures 1,739 metres (5,705 feet). The bedrock of the Porcupine Hills consists of Paleocene shales and sandstones. On the reserve, where the strata are horizontal, sandstone ridge tops are broad and relatively flat. The area is drained by three drainage basins with the Tennessee drainage being the most important. Numerous side coulees, arranged in a herringbone fashion drain into Tennessee Creek.

Topography alone (and resultant unsuitable soil-conditions) prohibits the cultivation of fieldcrops in most parts of the three Stoney Reserves and the Peigan Timber Limit (except the river bottom lands).

5.1.2 Climate

Looking at climatic conditions in terms of resource management we are interested in their impact on activities such as ranching, cropraising and forestry. For this purpose general conditions and mean values are of less importance than extremes, as the continental plains and foothills climate exhibits a high degree of variability.

The region is characterized by a BSk or "middle latitude dry" climate according to the Köppen-Trewartha classification. This means that the climate of the area is cool semi-arid, verging into cool subhumid in the foothills. The Peigan and the Stoney Reserves fall into a precipitation zone of 450-560 millimetres (18-22 inches) per annum, the Peigan Reserve tending to be on the drier side. The whole region shows a major peak in the precipitation distribution in June and a rapid drop in July (Fig. 4).

Figure 4: Mean monthly Temperature and Precipitation 1931-1960 for selected Centres in southern Alberta

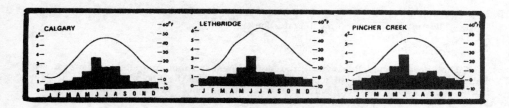

Sources: Adapted from Fletcher (1972), p. 21

In the foothills summer temperatures are moderate, and, therefore, the evaporation is relatively low. About 30 per cent of the annual precipitation occurs during the six winter months, October to March. Snow may account though for 40 per cent of the annual precipitation, and much of it falls in April which is the highest snowfall month (Kumar 1976: 10). While the snow is usually retained on the northern slopes it is cleared off the open southern slopes by Chinook winds, making winter pasture available. There is an ample and dependable water supply for livestock production in the region.

The contribution of snowpack to overall total precipitation is equally high on the Peigan Reserve, about 40 per cent. Summer rainfall (June to August) only contributes about one-third of the annual precipitation; and due to the warmer temperature the potential evapotranspiration in the prairies is much higher than in the foothills.

The winter climate in the foothills and prairies of southwestern Alberta is characterized by an alternation of cold, dry, rather still periods with periods of comparatively warm, dry, windy Chinook air, which gives the entire area a large winter temperature range. Extreme low temperatures occur when stable continental arctic air (northerlies, northwesterlies) stagnates over the eastern slopes of the Rockies and the western prairies. The Chinook is characterized by a strong westerly flow of air over the mountains with lee waves forming troughs and crests roughly parallel to the mountain ranges. The dry air descends the leeward side of the mountain and brings high temperatures and low humidities to the areas where the Chinook reaches the ground. But even though the Chinook is a regular feature of the southern Albertan climate, it cannot be relied upon by ranchers to make winter pasture available for their cattle every year. The year of 1906-1907 became known as "the year that the chinook did not come", when snow remained on the ground for the full length of the winter season and cattle starved to death by the tens of thousands. It is impossible to forecast the prevailing circulation for any winter, and the rancher must prepare himself by storing hay for extreme conditions without outside grazing.

Kumar (1976: 9) notes, that the red-belt conifer foliage injury occasionally observed on valley slopes outside the Stoney Reserve has been attributed to these abrupt alterations of cold arctic and warm Chinook air. The mean January temperature in the foothillfs is -12°C, while extremes of -50°C have been recorded. Generally this climate is suitable for winter recreation, although extremes can virtually nullify this (Underwood, McLellan and Associates Limited 1970: 10). The foothills summers are relatively cool with a mean maximum of about 23°C. The most illustrative climatic feature is perhaps the mean frostfree period, which for the Stoney Reserves is only forty to sixty days. This effectively limits the types of crops that can be grown, and in addition places severe limitations on the summer recreational potential, limiting the summer activity season to about 100 days from late May to early September.

With the general climatic pattern being similar conditions are slightly warmer on the Peigan Reserve. The mean January temperature is -9°C, but record lows of -42°C have been recorded as well. Chinooks are very frequent in this part of the prairies. Pincher Creek has recorded an average of forty Chinook days per winter. Exposed areas are usually swept clear of snow. This reduces the potential for cross-country skiing on ridge tops and grassy slopes on the Timber Limit (Synergy West 1975: 40). On the other hand, Fort Macleod experiences over 40 per cent of its winter days having temperatures above 5°C. Summers are warmer than in the foothills with a July mean maximum of 26°C: in each of the summer months June to August temperatures rise to over 30°C. In contrast to the Stoney Reserves, the area around Brocket is favoured by a frost-free period of 80-100 days.

Climate is only one of various factors which promote natural grasslands, but it is the predominant one (Carder 1970: 263). The grasslands characterizing the Peigan Reserve and parts of the Stoney Reserves are a response to summer drought. As outlined by Carder (1970) recurrent droughts favour the formation of cool-season grasses over trees. While their moisture requirement is critical in spring and early summer, they easily withstand late summer droughts, since grasses can aestivate during aridity and heat. Another important factor is the continentality of the climate, leading to an erratic amount and distribution of precipitation, both within the year and from year to year, and to equally violent changes in temperature. On the whole, grasses are better equipped than forest to withstand these erratic extremes. The same goes for their adaptation to strong, drying winds, the cold of the winter as well as the hot of summer. Even in southern Alberta, which is subject to the chinook, the warm wind of winter, trees can be winter-killed by desiccation, when soil water is made unavailable to them by frost. Concluding from long-term precipitation measurements on experimental farms, Lodge et al. (1971) point out that there is a fairly consistent pattern in the occurrence of dry and wet years all over the prairies. That means, if drought prevails at one site, then drier-than-average conditions are likely at the others, and thus there is little possibility of obtaining extra pasture in other districts (ibid.: 10). Second, there appears to be a cyclic pattern, as years of above average and below average precipitation occur together with fair regularity. Whereas one dry or wet year affects only the forage yield, a series of two or more dry or wet years influences the cover. Drought reduces the abundance of the higher-yielding grasses, whereas successive wet seasons lead to their increase. Thus the pattern of precipitation causes yields to vary so that forage may be in short supply or so plentiful that only a small portion of the yearly growth can be eaten - a fact which must be borne in mind with regard to stocking rates.

Treegrowth at higher elevations of the Stoney Reserves is in response to better availability of moisture, both edaphic and atmospheric. As it is common to most species, growth is better under conditions of greater humidity and less evaporation stress, but the dominant species, lodgepole pine and white spruce, thrive under a variety of climatic conditions. Douglas-fir is less prominent in the area but is found occasionally. All these conifers are adapted to an exceptionally wide range of temperature, especially lodgepole pine. The phenomenon called "red belt" was already mentioned: It means injury to needles by winter drying and seems to be associated with rapid temperature changes during winter when warm dry chinook winds replace frigid arctic air. The effect seems to be very localized, being most prevalent on slopes exposed to both wind and high radiation and less in protected areas (Satterlund 1973: 301). It is probably not caused just by high temperatures, but rather by excessive drying under a high heat load at a time when foliage moisture is not readily replaced.

The farmer faces much more stringent conditions due to climate than the rancher and forester. East of the foothills moisture supply is almost everywhere inadequate for high crop yields; therefore supplementary irrigation is utilized where practicable. Figure 5 shows the average water balance for the Lethbridge area. Although conditions on the Peigan Reserve are slightly moister due to the more westerly location, the same overall pattern applies. Potential evapotranspiration in the Lethbridge example is greater than precipitation for all months from April to October, but the deficiency is covered in May and June by moisture that entered the

Figure 5   Average Water Balance: Lethbridge, Alberta

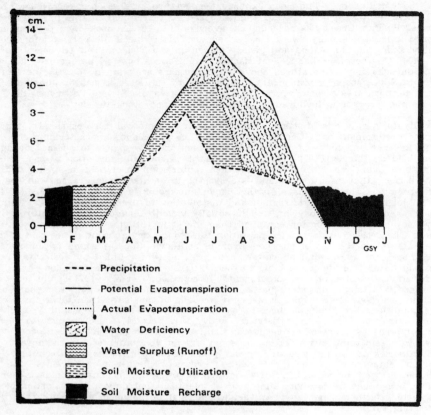

Sources: Adapted from Fletcher (1972), p. 30

soil during late fall and early spring. For high yields the crops in the region must be irrigated from June onward. The graph suggests that the soil moisture recharge occurs mostly during the winter months as well as late fall. Although some melt water enters the soil during periods of thawing temperatures, some remains as snow and the recharge is somewhat delayed. Wheat is the main crop grown under conditions of dry farming. Yields fluctuate greatly from year to year. The relationship between precipitation during the crop-year (September to August), mean temperature during the growing season (May to August), and wheat yield is shown in a climatograph (Fig. 6), again for the Lethbridge area. The graph's linear pattern illustrates the significance of precipitation in producing particular wheat yields. High yields occur when the precipitation amount lies between 330 and 510 millimetres (13-20 inches). Temperature plays a less significant role with the greatest yields corresponding to values of about 15°C (60°F). Most years warmer than average had above average wheat yields. Although there obviously is a causal relationship, year to year variability tends to be greater than suggested, primarily because of problems in obtaining accurate and comparable data over the sixty-three year period.

A variable and rather short frostfree period is another obstacle the farmer has to contend with. It has been partly overcome by the development of earlier maturing crops, but generally speaking, yields are normally inversely related to

Figure 6:   Climatograph: Wheat Yield (bushels per acre) after Summer Fallow, 1908-1970

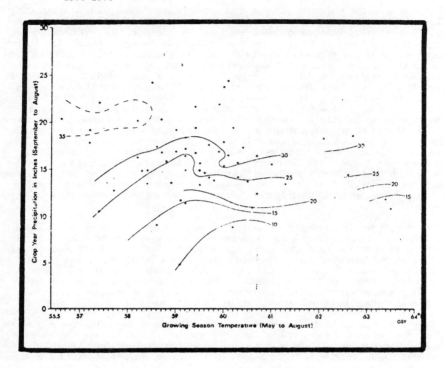

Sources: Adapted from Fletcher (1972), p. 31

early maturity, and short-growing-season crops such as barley are less valuable than wheat, for example.

Also precautions have to be taken against wind erosion. Especially a combination of relatively mild winters, light snow falls and subsequent strong spring winds is conducive to this hazard (Crown 1977: 3). Strip farming (alternating strips of cropped and fallowed land in a field) is considered to be a relatively inexpensive and efficient method of wind erosion control. For best results strips should be 100 metres (328 feet) wide, or less, and even narrower strips are required on certain soils. According to Crown (ibid.), a recent trend in southern Alberta, however, has been to much wider strips, probably because of the size of modern farm machinery and perhaps a complacent attitude toward wind erosion. The results have been dust storms and wind erosion for instance in the early springs of 1976 and 1977 reminiscent of the storms of the 1930s.

Finally, a hazard against which insurance is the only precaution the individual farmer can take, is hail. Moist air masses from the south, often interacting with air coming over the Rocky Mountains, form massive thunderclouds in the foothills and move eastwards over the prairies. On such occasions, damage to growing crops can be complete.

Thus it is not the severity of the climate, but its extreme variability, that imposes limits on both ranching and farming, and may even modify other practices such as forestry and outdoor recreation.

5.1.3 Soils

The soils of the Canadian prairies and adjacent parklands - an area including the Peigan Reserve and much of the Stoney Reserves - are of the chernozemic order. They have dark-coloured mineral-organic surface horizons and brownish, often prismatic subsurface horizons lying on calcareous parent material. The latter consists of glacial till, deposited by the Cordilleran glaciers in the foothills and adjacent western prairies during the Wisconsin glaciation. The easternmost limits of the effects of mountain glaciation lie approximately on a north-south line somewhere between Brocket and Fort Macleod; the main part of the southern Albertan plains falls under the influence of the Keewatin ice sheet. The chernozemic order includes three great groups - brown, dark brown and black - and some intrazonal types. The change in colour from brown to black reflects increasing soil moisture efficiency and accumulation of organic matter; it is an indication of the climate and vegetation under which these soils have developed. The Peigan and the (eastern) Stoney Reserves fall into the moister varieties of the chernozemic soils: On the Peigan Reserve soils vary between the dark brown and shallow black type, and the grass- and parklands of the Stoney Reserves bear black and degraded black soils (see map in Moss and Campbell 1947: 211). Local variations in parent material and drainage lead to the formation of solonetzic and gleysolic (meadow) soils within these major soil zones.

On the Morley Reserve proper shallow black soils are prominent in the eastern three quarters of the lowland area, whereas degraded grey-wooded soils (luvisolic order) characterize the western sector, the larger part of the Rabbit Lake Reserve and the Bighorn Reserve. The grey-wooded soils, here mostly on coarse till and till-colluvium mixture, have developed under cooler conditions where precipitation is more effective than on the grassland. Under undisturbed conditions they have a leaf litter accumulation on the surface over a distinct grey leached layer which in turn is underlain by a darker subsurface horizon enriched mainly in clay.

The Canada Land Inventory in its assessment of "Soil Capability for Agriculture" places the Stoney Reserves in the climatic subregion VCh, which is characterized by very severe limitations due to coolness. The soil-classes, identified by this system on the reserves, range from 5 to 7: climatic factors or adverse topography render these soils incapable of producing annual field crops. Class 6 soils, which cover a considerable part of the rangeland adjacent to the Bow River, do provide sustained grazing for livestock, but the limitations are considered so severe, that improvement of the forage production by the use of farm machinery - such as clearing of bush, cultivation, seeding, fertilizing - is deemed impractical. The level eastern extremity of the larger reserve is characterized by soils in class 5, where such improvement measures are feasible. Thus we can conclude, that the non-wooded or partially wooded areas - essentially the land east of Morley and a broad band along the Bow River west of Morley plus the Eden Valley Reserve - can be used only for grazing purposes and hay production.

The Peigan Reserve is characterized by black and dark brown chernozemic soils. As on the Stoney Reserves, the soils are generally quite fertile, and limitations to crop production are due to climatic conditions and terrain rather than soil characteristics. The Canada Land Inventory places the reserve into the climatic subregion IICa, which features "moderate limitations due to aridity". The soil classes, identified by this system on the reserve, range from 2 to 6 (Fig. 7). Large parts of the southwestern section of the reserve and some smaller areas of level terrain in the northwest fall into the capability class 2. This means moderate limitations that restrict the range of crops or require moderate conservation measures. Limitation is due to aridity. Class 3- soils cover large parts of the eastern reserve plus one large spot between the Number 3 Highway and the Oldman River. These soils have moderately severe limitations for crop-raising and require special conservation practices. Major limitations are due to inherent soil characteristics (3_S), for example undesirable structure, low permeability, restricted rooting zone, low natural fertility, low moisture holding capacity or salinity. Adverse topography (3_T) is another important limiting factor, especially in the steeper southeast and northwest. On the northeastern periphery severe erosion damage limits the potential (3_E).

Figure 7: Peigan Reserve: Soil Capability for Agriculture

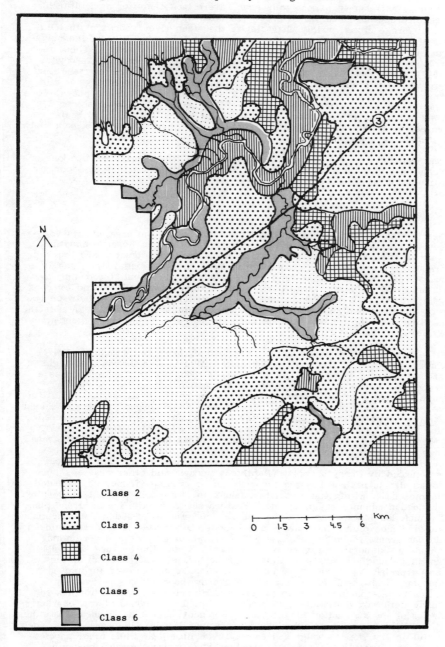

Class 2
Class 3
Class 4
Class 5
Class 6

Sources: Generalized after Canada Land Inventory: Soil Capability for Agriculture, Map 82H. Discussion see Text. C.N.

Patches of class 4-soils are found throughout the reserve, mainly 4_T (topographical limitations), but also 4_S. These soils have severe limitations for agricultural use and require special conservation practices. Soils in class 5 or 6, suited only for perennial forage crops, mainly characterize the steep river valleys of the Oldman River and Crowlodge Creek and the spurs of the Porcupine Hills in the northwest corner of the reserve. The Timber Limit falls into the same class. These results correspond to the overall findings of the Price-report (Price and Associates Limited 1967) which also places the main arable acreage into the southwestern part of the reserve. That study concludes that the greater part of the reserve is suitable for use as rangeland and about one-third is suitable for arable purposes. Today, 24,280 hectar (60,000 acres) out of the 42,350 hectar (104,650 acres) or 57 per cent are classified as rangeland, whereas out of the potential 16,190 hectar (40,000 acres) of arable land 4,047 hectar (10,000 acres have not been broken and are still used for grazing purposes.

We can conclude, that soil conditions alone do not impose major restrictions on resource use on either the Peigan or Stoney Reserves; problems that do occur are mainly attributable to climate and topography.

5.1.4 Vegetation

There is a close relationship between the soil zones of the area and its vegetation cover. The floral associations characterizing the Peigan Reserve and the eastern part of the main Morley Reserve and the Eden Valley Reserve are the fescue prairie (Festuca scabrella association of Moss and Campbell 1947) - the typical prairie of the black soil zone - and the parkland or grove belt (according to Moss 1932 and 1955). Whereas large parts of the Stoney lands are covered by parkland vegetation (Fig. 8), the Peigan Reserve is situated approximately between two ecotones or biotic tension zones: the prairie-forest ecotone in the west, towards the Porcupine Hills, and the tension zone between climax Festuca and Stipa associations (Mixed Prairie) in the east.

The Festuca scabrella association is described by Moss and Campbell (1947) as the climax grassland of the black soil zones of Alberta and also as the virgin prairie of the parkland belt. Moss (1932) does not recognize this association as a distinct type, but envisages the grassland of the grove belt as the "northern prairie" and regards Festuca scabrella merely as one of the chief components. With Moss and Campbell we must distinguish between the virgin fescue prairie, described as the Festuca scabrella association, and the so-called fescue grassland produced by mowing for hay or by moderate to heavy grazing. In the original fescue prairie, Festuca scabrella grows almost to the exclusion of other higher plants. This grass forms large bunches or tussocks from one to three feet high and ten to twenty inches in diameter. Where the soil is shallow or conditions are gravelly or rocky, fescue is replaced by Parry oatgrass (Danthonia parryi) and other grasses. The former seems also to replace Festuca scabrella under grazing. It may be regarded as an edaphic climax within the association (Moss and Campbell 1947: 212). Despite the pronounced dominance of one species, Festuca scabrella, the fescue grass plant community includes 148 species of higher plants: 20 grasses, 3 sedges, 10 shrubs and about 115 forbs plus a few mosses and lichens. Other associated grasses include wild oat grass, Idaho fescue, sheep fescue, wheat grasses and porcupine grass. Shrubby cinquefoil is a very common shrub. Today the Festuca scabrella association in its original form is confined to relict areas. Practically all of the virgin fescue prairie has been either broken or considerably altered through mowing or grazing. As a result of mowing of the grass, the main species Festuca scabrella has become much smaller in stature and diameter of tussock but has remained fairly uniformly distributed. Between the bunches, several of the "characteristic" species of the association have become prominent, and some species from other communities of the region have established themselves locally. On poorer sites, such as stony soil or dry slopes, rough fescue may even disappear while other species become abundant, notably Idaho fescue (Festuca idahoensis), western porcupine grass (Stipa spartea var. curtiseta), northern wheatgrass (Agropyron dasystachyum), junegrass (Koeleria cristata) and certain forbs. Parry oatgrass is dominant in local-

Figure 8: Morley Reserve: Distribution of Grassland and Forest Land

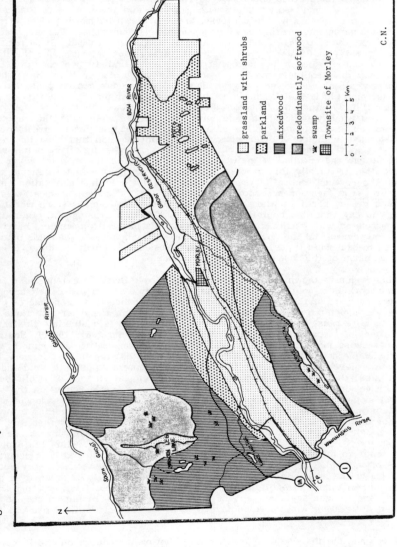

Sources: Fig. 4-15 in Western Research and Dev. Ltd. (1980) and Fig. 1 in Bailey (1964); Topographical Maps 820/2 and 820/3 East Series A 741; aerial photographs (see p. 255); field reconnaissance.

ized areas, especially on exposed wind-blown slopes, as for example in the southern part of the Porcupine Hills. Standard mowing practice for fescue grassland in Alberta is to take a crop of hay in alternate years. Under these conditions a good area will yield about one ton per acre in the year taken. Grazing of Festuca scabrella has a somewhat different effect from that of mowing, in that this grass becomes quite patchy, tending to persist on moister sites and where given some protection from grazing animals by small woody plants. Succeeding plants of rough fescue on better sites are slender wheatgrass (Agropyron trachycaulum), junegrass, Hooker's oatgrass (Avena Hookeri), western porcupine grass and intermediate oatgrass (Danthonia intermedia). On drier sites junegrass, Idaho fescue, Parry oatgrass, northern wheatgrass and some Poa (blue grass) species become quite common. Sedges, too, increase markedly with grazing, and the same goes for many of the shrubs and forbs, which in contrast, are kept down by mowing. The effect of heavy or indiscriminate grazing can be the complete elimination of Festuca scabrella and the "take-over" by more xeric species like needle-and-thread (Stipa comata) and blue grama (Bouteloua gracilis). These grasses (characteristic for the light brown soil zone) do occur in the fescue region under undisturbed conditions, but only on very dry, south-facing slopes or certain kinds of clay flats. From there these less vigorous and lower-yielding plants spread to overgrazed pastures. A significant example is the dominance of blue grama grass on the east side of the Porcupine Hills. A study by Johnston, Dormaar and Smoliak (1971) of fescue grassland soils at Stavely indicates that under heavy grazing along with the vegetation cover the soil is also changed: The character of the original fescue grassland soil is transformed to that of a drier microclimate, a phenomenon that must be borne in mind with regard to chances of rehabilitation. Thus overgrazing of the native rangeland results in the creation of artificial "droughty" conditions in plant cover and soil formation. Naturally this process is particularly effective in the tension zone between the Festuca scabrella association and the Mixed Prairie association (its Stipa-Agropyron faciation according to Coupland 1961: dominant species: western porcupine grass, northern wheatgrass, needle-and-thread and western wheatgrass). Needless to say that this boundary is dynamic. Through grazing and other disturbances associated with settlement of the region, this natural tension line has been shifted considerably to the north and west. Far more conspicuous than this boundary between two grassland types, however, is the grassland-woodland ecotone, evidenced by the invasion of the fescue grassland by aspens.

This region is known as "Parkland" or the "Grove Belt". It extends as a fringe along the foothills of southern Alberta and northeastward as a broad belt across the south-central part of the province. Its typical appearance is as a mosaic of prairie patches and aspen groves, with fescue prairie occupying the drier situations and aspen the more moist and sheltered places. This pattern is a striking illustration of the effect of topography on plant succession (Coupland 1961: 160 f): South-facing slopes cause increased aridity because of higher temperature and runoff, whereas north-facing slopes are protected from the sun so that the habitat is more humid than even on level land. Similarly, western slopes are more exposed to wind than are eastern ones, the drying effect probably being strongest on tops of knolls because of higher velocity. These factors permit the survival of xeric relicts on the south and west slopes and on knoll tops and respectively survival or intrusion of mesic vegetation on north and east slopes. Transition from parkland, whether to open prairie or to forest, is usually gradual. Moss (1932: 404) emphasizes that this broad transition belt actually contains within it thousands of true tension lines or ecotones, these occurring wherever poplar and prairie communities meet. Thus the aspen vegetation tends to invade and to succeed the prairie vegetation, and as a result, the borders of individual aspen groves become composed of trees considerably younger than those of the main body of the stand (sometimes also to be explained as a consequence of burnings of the marginal part of the grove). Counteracting this tendency are various agencies such as burning, browsing/grazing, damage by rabbits, and desiccating winds, which favor the prairie association and prevent the aspen from occupying the drier situations.

Trees and shrubs also dominate the river bottom community on the Peigan Reserve: narrow-leaf cottonwood (Populus trichocarpa) and balsam poplar (Populus balsamifera) with an understory of birch (Betula spp.), willow (Salix spp.) and snowberry (Symphericarpos Duhamel). These plant communities are maintained by the relative instability of their habitat and constitute seral communities (early stages in plant succession). They exist because of the "constant erosion, deposition and channel shifting by the rivers" (Brayshaw 1965: 9).

The Peigan Timber Limit lies in a broad transition zone where five vegetation types meet and, therefore, is characterized by a complex floral mosaic (Synergy West Limited 1975: 10). The Montane forest of the southern Canadian Rocky Mountains, the Upper Foothills forest of the west, the fescue grassland and the aspen parkland of the foothills/prairie transition all mingle in the Porcupine Hills. In their southern part, on 147B, this pattern is slightly modified by the predominant presence of Douglas-fir (Pseudotsuga menziesii, Franco var. glauca) in coniferous stands. On south facing slopes, where the grass is interrupted by occasional sandstone outcroppings, open stands of limber pine (Pinus flexilis) are also found.

The grey-wooded soil areas of the Stoney Reserves - higher elevations of the western Morley Reserve, Rabbit Lake and Bighorn - are timbered (Fig. 8). The Morley Reserve lies largely within the Douglas-Fir and Lodgepole Pine Section of the Montane Forest Region (M 5 after Rowe 1972: 77). Lodgepole pine (Pinus contorta Dougl. var. latifolia) white spruce (Picea glauca), Douglas-fir and trembling aspen (Populus tremuloides) are the principal species found. Lodgepole pine and poplar are subclimax, fire succession species, and their widespread distribution attests to the high incidence of forest fires in the foothills in former times. White spruce, on the other hand, is a climax species of the region. Douglas-fir is limited in extent and of little economic value. According to Bailey (1964: 1), lodgepole pine and white spruce account for 60 per cent of the total merchantable volume and 90 per cent of the marketable volume. Hardwood species, primarily poplar, form one-third of the total volume but have very limited marketability. The most productive stands of softwood timber are concentrated in the southern part of the Morley Reserve on valley slopes with a northern exposure. This concentration is doubtlessly attributable to the northerly aspect which aids in conserving moisture. The best sites are found on the lower moist slopes and in the deep soiled portions of drainage channels giving protection from dry chinook winds. Lodgepole pine and white spruce are also abundant in the northwestern part of the reserve (Ghost River block), but growth is poor due to immature soils and frequent fires. Poplar occurs throughout the reserve but grows especially on the south-facing valley slopes to the north of the Bow River, and also north of Chiniki Lake.

The Rabbit Lake Reserve falls into the Upper Foothills Section of the Boreal Forest Region (B19c after Rowe 1972: 40). Lodgepole pine is the dominant species and is found in pure stands or mixed with white spruce. Pure poplar stands occur at lower elevations. As on the Morley Reserve deciduous trees concentrate on the warmer, southern slopes, and at lower elevations, while coniferous stands predominate on the cool, northern slopes and at higher elevations. Extensive muskeg areas characterize the depression containing Rabbit Lake in the west of the reserve. Lodgepole pine is the dominant species in the central part of the reserve where it occurs in almost pure stands, whereas in the eastern half it is mixed with poplar and white spruce.

The forest on the Bighorn Reserve belongs to the same type as the Rabbit Lake area. White spruce is more frequent here than lodgepole pine and constitutes 52 per cent of the total merchantable volume compared to 37 per cent in the case of the latter. Both are found in pure and mixed stands. Aspen occur on the lower elevations. There are scattered balsam firs (Abies balsamea) on the higher ridges in the reserve.

The forest resource lends itself to other uses besides timber harvesting such as outdoor recreation, that can be incorporated in a multiple use framework, as will be shown in subsequent chapters.

5.1.5   Geology

The elements discussed in the previous chapters - relief, climate, soils and vegetation - altogether constitute the renewable resource sector. On the other hand, non-renewable resources arising from the geological characteristics of the area form another very important component of the land-based economy of the reserves.

The major non-agricultural resources of the area are the fossil fuels: coal, petroleum and natural gas. The bulk of the oil and gas accumulations in western Canada occurs in stratigraphic traps (Norris and Bally 1972: 16). Oil migrates outwards and upwards from its source beds - such as clay and shale, now compact and impervious - and passes into porous or fissured reservoir beds, for example sandstone or limestone, then rises to the highest possible level, and collects into an oil pool wherever the structure provides a trap which impedes further migration. Gas, if present in excess of the amount that the oil can hold in solution, bubbles to the top and forms a gas cap over the oil pool. There are a variety of types of structural traps (Fig. 9) such as anticlines (a), lenses of porous material within shales (c), or the upper ends of tilted reservoir beds cut off by some impervious barrier. The obstacle may be a fault throwing an impervious bed against the reservoir bed (b), or a hill belonging to an ancient land surface which was unconformably overlapped and buried by a younger series of petroliferous strata (d), or a salt dome which has perforated and ascended through a thick series of sediments (e) or an erosional unconformity. Oil need not be confined to a single reservoir bed in a given field. Any suitably placed formation may have been fed either from an outlying primary source, or via an underlying pool, the oil from which escaped upwards through fractures in the intervening impervious beds. Gas, in particular, easily migrates to higher levels, and in places vast quantities have accumulated as buried "gas fields". This reflects the natural tendency of some varieties of petroleum to differentiate into asphaltic and gaseous fractions. If the original reservoirs begin to leak after such fractionation has taken place, the mobile gas moves on and leaves the sticky asphalt behind. Such may have been the case in the southern part of the province, where natural gas production generally overshadows petroleum (Beaty 1972: 18 f).

When related to the oil and gas output of Alberta as a whole, the region in which the Stoney and Peigan Reserves are located, cannot be regarded as a major producing area. The major oil and gas fields of the province are found in the basin of sedimentary rock known as the Alberta Synkline. Wide open structures surrounded by extensive gathering grounds have a much better chance of being productive than more closely packed folds. The Peigan and Stoney lands lie over the Foothills geologic province, where the strata are greatly twisted and folded, and very intensive exploration is needed to locate the reservoirs. Nevertheless, the eastern part of the Morley Reserve is underlain by a large gas field, the Jumping Pound West Field, with the Jumping Pound Field in close proximity outside the reserve. In the eastern half of the Rabbit Lake Reserve the Stoneys also participate in the Wildcat Hills Field. The gas occurs in narrow thrust structures involving Mississippian carbonate rocks of the Turner Valley Member at the top of the Livingstone Formation. The reservoirs are in partially dolomitized limestones. A number of smaller fields is being exploited further west on the reserve, such as the Ghost Field and the Morley Field.

No exploitable reservoir is known yet underneath the Peigan Reserve. But in close proximity we find the Pincher Creek Gas Field; like in Jumping Pound West the main reservoir is dolomite of the Turner Valley Member of the Livingstone Formation at a drilling depth of almost 4,000 metres (13,128 feet). The Pincher Creek Field is regarded as one of the major gas fields of its kind in the world based on its reserves of natural gas, sulphur, condensate, propane and butane. Other fields in the area are the Waterton Gas Field and the Lookout Butte Field.

Compared to the oil and gas potential other minerals are of minor importance to the reserves. According to Carlson (1980), thin coal seams may be present beneath the Peigan Reserve within Cretaceous age strata including the St. Mary

Figure 9: Sections to illustrate various types of structural traps favourable to the accumulation of oil and gas (gas is omitted exept in (a)) Discussion in Text.

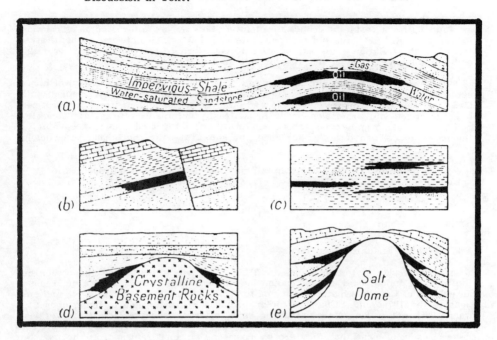

Sources: Adapted from Holmes (1965), p. 455

River, Belly River, Cardium and Kootenay Formations. The depth of burial of these formations, however, is beyond economic limits for surface mining and underground methods. In the late 1970s exploratory drilling on the main reserve intersected thin coal seams within the Belly River Formation at 1,350 metres (4,429 feet) and the Kootenay Formation at 2,800 metres (15,748 feet). Present mining technology limits open pit mining depths to less than 60 metres (197 feet). Therefore, the Peigans' coal seams are of no economic significance for the time being, but there may be economic potential in the future when new technologies are developed and in the face of rising energy prices. Extensive glacio-fluvial deposits of sand and gravel are located on terraces along the Oldman River, but due to the lack of a foreseeable market for these commodities they are neither being utilized nor have they been explored to any extent.

On the Stoney Reserves there is a chance of the existence of coal seams of commercial value underneath the Bighorn Reserve, but the potential can be determined only by extensive test drilling. Gravel deposits of commercial value are found on all reserves except the Bighorn. Lime and clay provide a basis for a cement plant on the main Morley Reserve.

5.2 The Factors of Production: Land, Labour and Capital

In their "Agricultural Geography" (London 1971) Morgan and Munton propose the following economic agents as factors of production: land, labour and capital. The validity of this statement is not confined to the agricultural sector only, but it seems applicable to the land-based economiy in general, be it renewable or non-renewable resources. As the authors base their text on the European and Anglo-American situation, we have to ask ourselves whether these economic agents need to be redefined for the Native American context.

In the previous chapter "land" was introduced as the bearer of certain natural attributes with a resultant economic potential. Now we are interested in its relation to Man who utilizes it for his purposes. We can distinguish between a quantitative aspect of this relation - the amount of land compared to the population it carries - and a qualitative aspect - the kind of land tenure involved.

According to Morgan and Munton (op.cit.: 16) "labour" represents "all human services other than decision making". Life in white society is highly compartmentalized; the economy is disassociated from all other activities and in itself corporatized, bureaucratized and professionalized. In contrast, in Indian cultures the economic, political, religious and social sphere constitute one integrated whole. Accordingly, the narrowly defined term "labour" shall be substituted by the human potential in the widest possible sense.

The definition of the term "capital" as "the non-labour resources" (ibid.) applies here without modification.

5.2.1 The Land

5.2.1.1 Land: an unresolved Issue

A discussion of Indian lands would be incomplete without some elaboration on the topic of Indian land claims. Indian land claims have been a feature of almost all periods of Canada's history, but due to legal and political factors (1) it has only been in the 1970s and 1980s that Indian people were really able to bring claims forward. With native land claims affecting such different issues as the controversies over the patriation of the Canadian Constitution and northern development projects, it becomes very clear that they are by no means an anachronism from the past but unfinished business that demands to be taken care of.

There are various types of claims. So-called comprehensive claims concern native people who never signed land-cession treaties with the Crown (in the Maritimes, Quebec, British Columbia, Yukon and parts of the Northwest Territories) and are based on aboriginal rights (2). They do not concern us here, Then there are specific claims based on law ful obligations; these may be claims for lands due to native people as part of a treaty agreement with the Crown, or they may involve lost land, surrendered under often dubious circumstances since the creation of the reserves.

The vital importance Indian people ascribe to their landbase cannot be overemphasized. Marie Marule (1978: 111) speaks for most Treaty Indians when she states: "The elimination of reserve lands inevitably means the termination of status and rights for Indian people. The easiest way to destroy the distinctiveness of Indian people and their cultural heritage is to eliminate the land base." While today strong economic interests are at stake especially in Alberta, most Indians still view

---

1) For details see Daniel, R.C., 1980, A History of Native Claims Processes in Canada, 1867-1979, prepared by R.C. Daniel, Tyler, Wright & Daniel Limited, Research Consultants for Research Branch, Department of Indian and Northern Affairs.
2) "Aboriginal rights" are those property rights which inure to native peoples by virtue of their occupation of certain lands from time immemorial. For more detail see Cumming, P.A. and N.H. Mickenberg, eds., 1972, Native Rights in Canada, Toronto, pp. 13-50. A more philosophical interpretation is presented by Harold Cardinal, 1977, The Rebirth of Canada's Indians, Edmonton, pp. 136-145.

their land as much more than a piece of real estate. Constant assaults on this land base on the part of the government through repeated amendments of the Indian Act and, more recently, through the White Papier, have bred an attitude of distrust among Indians wherever land is concerned, and not surprisingly the land question remains an unresolved issue with both the Stoneys and Peigan in various cases. Some of these date back to the days of Treaty Seven, others were caused by more recent developments.

The Wesley Stoneys' Bighorn-Kootenay Plains land claim is an example for the former. It will be remembered from Chapter 3 that the northern Stoney Band's territory was not covered by Treaty Seven, and that after the establishment of the Morley Reserve one-third of this band under Moosekiller (Peter Wesley after whom the band was named henceforward) moved out of the reserve and back to their ancestral hunting grounds along the banks of the North Saskatchewan River in 1894. When they launched their first petition for a reserve in the North Saskatchewan headwaters to the Department of Indian Affairs, in 1909, Alberta had already provincial status (since 1905), while control of Crown lands was still retained by the federal government. In 1910 the Indian Affairs Branch actually accepted the Indians' claim, first merely their need of more (agricultural and grazing, not hunting according to Indian Affairs) land, but finally even the location on the Kootenay Plains. Consequently the Department of Indian Affairs approached the Minister of the Interior requesting the release of Crown land at Kootenay Plains to be converted into an Indian reserve. In the following year, though, the Department suddenly reversed its decision and rejected the request. The reason given for its refusal was that permanent Indian settlement in the upper North Saskatchewan Valley would result in the extermination of wildlife. According to Larner (1976: 88) the true reason behind it rather was anticipated economic development, illustrated by the Geological Survey's involvement with commercial interests seeking mineral concessions in the Bighorn Valley. The subsequent policy seems to verify this. In any case the Forestry Branch of the federal Department of the Interior was another force instrumental in opposing Indian establishment at Kootenay Plains. In 1910 the Rocky Mountain Forest Reserve had been created, encompassing the entire eastern slope of Alberta. The Forestry Branch, charged with its management, was looking for good hay or grazing lands where it could position its rangers. Due to their central location within the Forest Reserve the Kootenay Plains were particularly attractive for this purpose. As a result, within the Ministry of the Interior there were two branches vying for the Kootenay Plains: Indian Affairs and Forestry (Snow 1977: 77). No agreement between the conflicting interests was reached, and the conflict was left in abeyance for a couple of years, especially because the Kootenay Stoneys were independent of the ration house.

The majority pursued the traditional semi-nomadic way of life, but people had also built houses, planted gardens and owned numerous horses and cattle. Over one hundred head of cattle were even moved from Morley to the plains because of the deteriorated grazing conditions on the reserve. The Stoneys had been permitted by forestry officials to use forestry ranches, upon payment of the usual fee, and the provincial Department of Agriculture had even issued them licenses to hunt in the regular open season (Snow 1977: 84). Yet they were still regarded as squatters, and in 1915 Indian Affairs and the Forestry Branch jointly embarked upon a program of forcible removal and subsequent compensation of the Kootenay Plains Indians. Action was going to be taken in 1918, but Indian Commissioner Graham's objection, that the reserve was unable to sustain 200 head of cattle, drought conditions prevailing, resulted in an indefinite postponement of the plan (Larner 1976: 89) and its final abandonment. Thus the Stoneys were again encouraged, albeit obliquely, to stick to their ancestral lands.

When the 1930 Natural Resources Act transferred the natural resources or more specifically the Crown lands from the federal to the provincial government, the chances of being granted a reserve within the Clearwater Forest Reserve were even further reduced, and Ottawa was in a position to conveniently rid itself of any responsibility. Likewise, however, there was no attempt to remove the people to Morley, and they were free to stay and continue using traplines registered with the province. Yet eventually, mainly due to the initiative of John Laurie, then Secretary of the Indian Association of Alberta, in 1947 the Province of Alberta agreed to cooperate with the federal government in making a 2,024 hectar (5,000 acre) tract available to the Stoneys as a reserve, though not on the Kootenay Plains but at the confluence of the Bighorn and North Saskatchewan rivers. It is impossible within the scope of this chapter to elaborate on all the inadequacies and dissensions occurring during the procedure not only between Ottawa and Edmonton but also between the Department of Indian Affairs and its own field staff. It must suffice to say, that the acreage envisaged was not even capable of accommodating the present number of horses and cattle not to speak of developing a ranching or farming economy with the production of winter feed. Using the land/people ratio of Treaty Seven of one square mile or 640 acres per five persons, the reserve land should have been in the neighbourhood of 5,180 hectar (12,800 acres) rather than 2,024 hectar (5,000 acres). Hence it is no surprise, that the Indians attending the meetings on this subject in 1947 apparently believed all the time (and were given the impression) that additional land was forthcoming, that the Bighorn Reserve was just "a waiting place" (Snow 1977: 89; Larner 1976: 89). In the summer of 1948 an Order-in-Council was passed establishing the special Bighorn Reserve 144A. In the official document particular emphasis was placed on two points: that the Stoney band had no claim to the land in question, having already received land grants consistent with the terms of Treaty Seven, and that the mineral rights would be withheld from them. There was an awareness of the great mineral potential in the North Saskatchewan Valley.

After the Natural Resources Act the federal government had given up any effective enforcement of the treaty Indians' right to hunt and fish in unoccupied crown land. By and large the Albertan government kept the agreement that the Stoneys were allowed hunting in the Rocky Mountain Forest Reserve, but it introduced an increasing number of restrictions. In the transfer agreement in 1947 one such matter was the condition that the number of Indian horses should be reduced to a minimum in order to get rid of the wild or semi-wild horses roaming provincial lands (and eating up valuable hay). Accordingly, in the 1950s, Dominion and provincial forestry officials systematically rounded up and killed horses at Bighorn-Kootenay Plains, many of them Stoney horses. For the Indians this ment a considerable economic loss, since these animals were not only trained for hunting and trapping purposes but also constite a "mobile bank". At the same time the upper North Saskatchewan Valley was thrown open to the major North American oil corporations for seismographic surveys resulting in hundreds of miles of seismic cuts crisscrossing the entire region (Larner 1976: 89). Simultaneously service access roads were cut through the valley. Large and small game were driven from the district by all these activities, while the Bighorn Stoneys as well as those residing at Morley suffered extreme loss of food and fur trapping income.

The fatal blow to whatever was left of the Bighorn Stoneys' self-sufficiency was dealt at them by the provincial government and Calgary Power Limited in the early 1970s with the construction of the Bighorn Dam on the North Saskatchewan River immediately above the Bighorn Stoney lease tract. The Stoneys and the Indian Association of Alberta had tried in vain to prevent the implementation of this hydroelectric project. The 43-kilometre (27-mile) man-made lake has inundated virtually the entire claim area of Kootenay Plains, flooding cabins, graves, campgrounds and pastures. Morever, it extinguished the Stoneys' livelihood derived from hunting, guiding hunters and trapping fur animals. About 95 per cent of the Bighorn Stoneys who used to be the most self-reliant section of the tribe, have been on welfare since the completion of the dam in 1972.

When the Stoneys realized in 1969 that any further attempts to prevent the construction of the dam would be futile, they decided, instead, to try once again to get the government to acknowledge and guarantee the rights of the Bighorn Indians and to assist the Bighorn people to adapt to the changes that would result from the construction of the dam. They requested the provincial government to compensate them for any losses due to the effects of the dam. This compensation included financial assistance to help establish economic projects and job training programs, but the main thrust was to get a reserve established in the Kootenay Plains area. The provincial government's reaction was, that if there was to be any meaningful settlement, particularly if this settlement involved land, the Stoneys would have to prove legal entitlement to the land. Equally, the federal government saw itself in a position, where it could only respond to a legal claim since all complaints and problems relating to the dam were a matter of provincial jurisdiction. This ruling gave rise to the Research Report by Getty and Larner (1972). The Indian Affairs department provided the Stoneys with $ 30,000 to conduct this oral and documentary study of their entitlement to land in the Kootenay Plains area (1). Even while the research was still being conducted, the provincial government indicated that, if the federal government acknowledged that there was an outstanding treaty claim of land, it would not hesitate to provide the land as it was obliged to do by the terms of the 1930 Natural Resources Act (2) (Getty 1975: 67). Moreover, after the reservoir was filled, five square kilometres (two square miles) of land were turned over to the Stoneys as compensation for the loss of a religious and cultural area, but with the stipulation, that this new area could only be used for cultural, religious or historical purposes (Fig. 10). The federal government was presented with the Kootenay Plains land research report in April 1972. Both the Stoneys and the federal government had asked Dr. Barber, Indian Claims Commissioner, to evaluate the findings. In the fall of 1972, he recommended to the Department of Indian Affairs that the research report confirmed that the Bighorn Wesley band did have an unfulfilled claim to treaty land in the Bighorn district, and that the federal government should settle the claim as soon as possible. For fear of establishing a precedent that could lead to claims from other bands across Canada, there was considerable stalling on the part of the government, but finally, in January 1974, the Department of Indian Affairs officially acknowledged that the Bighorn Stoneys should be given reserve land in the district in settlement of an unfulfilled treaty land claim.

Treaty Seven provided that one square mile of land be given for each family of five persons. The problem now arising was what date should be selected to determine the population figure: 1877 when the treaty was signed; the early 1900s when the federal government first promised to establish a reserve in that area; 1948 when the existing small reserve was set aside; or the present-day census figure, when the terms of the treaty were to be honoured. After lengthy negotiations a population figure of 144 persons resident on the reserve as of December 31, 1972, was finally agreed upon. This translated into a reserve of approximately 7,285 hectar (18,000 acres).

Now, apparently all that remained to be done was for the provincial government to provide the land requested, as spelled out by the laws of the province. Instead, after further delays, the Government of Alberta declared that it rejected the federal government's request to provide the land to meet the outstanding treaty obligation. They were going to place the case before the court to challenge the legality of the Stoney claim in spite of the fact that the Indian Claims Commissioner and the federal government had already acknowledged its validity. On December 2, 1977, the Wesley Band formally filed a claim with the federal government. To date, more than four years later, the question is still before the courts.

An interesting question that can only be speculated upon is whether things might have taken a different turn if environmental and social impact assessment

---

1) This was the first time the Department of Indian Affairs had provided any kind of a grant to an Indian band to help them carry out research on treaty rights. Since that time, the department has provided some research funds to other Indian bands and organizations.
2) The Natural Resources Act provided for the ownership of all Crown land (except National Parks and Indian Reserves) to be transferred to the provincial government. One of the provisions of the Act though, stipulates that if at any time in the future the federal government was obliged to provide reserve land for an Indian band to fulfill a treaty commitment, the province would provide unoccupied Crown land for this purpose. However, this provision does not indicate what the federal government would have to give in return for the new reserve land, nor does it stipulate that the province has to provide the specific land requested.

Figure 10: The Bighorn-Kootenay Plains Land Claim

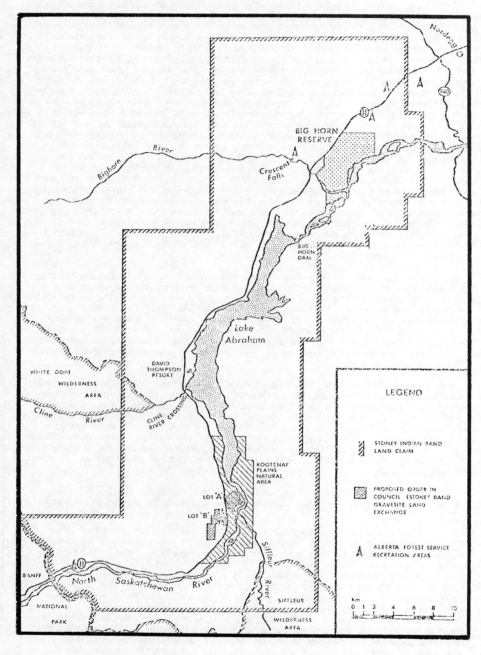

Sources: Adapted from Howard (1979), Figure 4

legislation had been in the 1960s what it is today. As Howard (1979: 131) points out, during the planning of the dam no assessment of the social and environmental costs was ever made. Certain economic costs were also excluded from the assessment, including the cost of road construction, bridge and campground redevelopment, and the cost of land clearing. Had these been included in the cost-estimate of the project (as today's more intensive economic analysis would have required) it is possible that the dam would not even have been built given the alternative of expanding the thermal-generating plant at Wabamun. The fact that there were no public hearings prior to the construction of the dam further removed any objections to the project from public and political processes of review. The expectations of the public in participating in the development and conservation of the environment have risen since the 1960s. Although it is questionable whether the issue of native land claims would have been addressed in the context of social impact assessment - despite the important precedent for doing so set by Justice Thomas Berger - a somewhat more humane treatment of the Stoneys would likely have occurred, given formal impact assessment.

Another observation, made also by using the knowledge and vision of hindsight, is that the Stoneys' unwillingness to use pressure tactics considerably weakened their bargaining position (Getty 1975) because the government knew that they could delay and procrastinate without having to worry about any negative repercussions. The Bighorn people could have organized boycotts, demonstrations, sit-ins, picket lines, or even tried to obtain a court injunction to stop construction. All these kinds of tactics would have focused public attention upon the problem and, to whatever degree they were successful, it would have increased pressure on the government. Instead, the Stoneys chose to trust the government without having the means to make them live up to their promises. This is particularly interesting in the light of what was going to happen at the Peigan weir a few years later (see p. 42).

The Bighorn-Kootenay Plains land claim may be the most serious grievance the Stoneys have, but it is not the only one. Another question which is still in the courts is the problem of mineral rights in the highway exchange land. When the Transcanada Highway was constructed in 1961 and widened in 1968, using reserve lands, the Stoneys received surface rights to land in the Broken Leg Lake area and Jumping Pound area plus a small addition to the Rabbit Lake Reserve in exchange for the highway right-of-way (fig. 11). The Stoneys feel that building a major highway across their land amounts to the same as giving up the mineral rights, and therefore they demand them in the new land.

An issue that was settled out of court was the United Church land claim. It involved 87 hectar (216 acres) of land originally claimed by Reverend George McDougall's Mission, but also claimed by the Stoney tribe as their land. Just over 16 hectar (40 acres) have been designated as a historic site (including a replica of the old mission church, east of Morley), thus falling under provincial guidelines and still registered with the United Church of Canada. There are plans (in the planning and fund raising stage) to develop an interpretive centre on the site, a project where the Stoneys have been invited to participate. After lengthy negotiations between the United Church and the band council the remaining land reverted to the Stoneys in 1979.

With the Peigan Tribe, a contentious issue which was settled only recently, stemmed from the question of who owns the Oldman River waterbed. The fact that - in contrast to the United States - with regard to Indian Reserves there is no generally applicable water right in Canada, renders water-related questions particularly complicated. In 1979, the Peigan became involved in a dispute with the Province of Alberta (and by implication with the Lethbridge Northern Irrigation District, L.N.I.D.) regarding that part of the L.N.I.D. system which runs through the reserve and which includes a diversion weir, a canal and a flume. The Peigan were contending that these facilities were located on unexpropriated land and therefore were in place illegally. They asked the Province of Alberta to pay them compensation retroactively for the presence of these facilities on what they perceived as Band lands and also that a yearly fee system be inaugurated for each acre of land irrigated by the L.N.I.D. system. When these demands were not met, in April

Figure 11: The Composition of Stoney Land

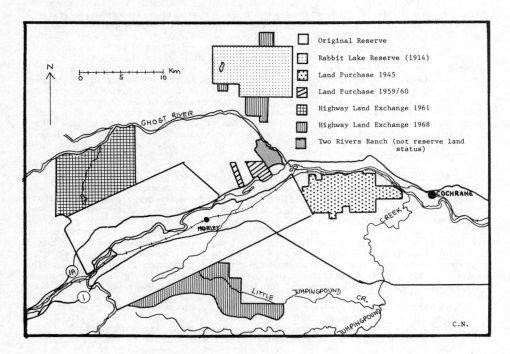

Sources: Stoney Tribal Administration

1979 the Peigan set up a blockade on the Oldman River and refused to allow officials of the L.N.I.D. to open the flood gates, thus cutting off water from 54,000 irrigation-dependent hectars (133,000 acres) and domestic water to 900 farms and 7 communities north of Lethbridge. After one month, the Peigan finally lifted their blockade and resorted to diplomatic negotiations with the provincial government. The result was a temporary agreement, consisting in a cash settlement of $ 435,000 with the Alberta government, giving them access to the irrigation headworks for the next two years.

This being only a temporary access permit, negotiations with the provincial government were resumed the following year. After nine months a memorandum of agreement was drafted and signed (pending a formal agreement) to the effect that in exchange for a cash settlement of $ 2.5 million plus an amount each year equivalent to the annual compounded interest on $ 1 million the province be provided with land for the headworks and main canal of the L.N.I.D., road access, plus land for a construction site to expand and repair the irrigation system. Yet, in early February 1981, a stalemate was reached with the Peigan growing suspicious over the wording used in the memorandum. The agreement stipulated in part that the provincial government would have "proprietary interest" in certain portions of land needed for irrigation weir expansion, whereas the Peigan Chief and Council were only prepared to grant them a landuse permit for the land involved for the life of the irrigation works. It took five more months for both parties to come to a final and satisfactory agreement ending the three year dispute over water rights on the Oldman River. The province agreed to pay the Peigan $ 4 million, plus an annual cash payment of $ 300,000 for the life of the water diversion system on Indian land. In exchange, the Peigan dropped all past grievances and granted the province landuse permits for 83 hectar (204 acres) of canal right-of-way, for 1.6 hectar (4 acres) of river bed on which the diversion weir and flume are situated, and 21 hectar (51 acres) for reconstruction and expansion of the system, plus road access from Highway No. 3 to the weir site with the provision that the Department of Environment maintain the road.

In many ways the accomplishment of this "deal" constitutes a landmark in the dealings between the government and an Indian Band. The land subject to dispute was expropriated in 1921 by the federal government. The Peigan claim that the government did not have the jurisdiction to complete this expropriation. The land and the facilities thereon have been used for irrigation purposes ever since; but their management was transferred from the federal government to the Province of Alberta only in 1976. With the recognition of their rights to the Oldman River waterbed the Peigan won the first major land claims settlement in Western Canada. Another breakthrough was their successful resistance to an expropriation by means of a land surrender and subsequent lease in favour of a permit system, where the band retains ownership of the land in question and regains control when/ if the L.N.I.D. works are no longer needed. Section 28 of the Indian Act provides that a permit may be issued allowing a non-band member to occupy or use reserve lands. If the permit is for less than one year it can be issued on the authority of the Minister (of Indian Affairs) alone. If it is for longer than one year, it can only be issued by the Minister with the consent of the band council. There is no express limitation in the section on either the duration of the permit (providing the band council has consented) or on the use of land which can be allowed. The current policy of the department, however, is much more restrictive. The Department will not issue permits in situations where, in other contexts, a lease could be seen as the normal method of handling the rights. In order for reserve land to be leased, the band must surrender the land to the Crown whereupon the federal government leases the land to the non-band member. Section 38(2) of the Indian Act provides that a surrender may be "absolute or qualified, conditional or unconditional". There are no ground rules in the Indian Act or in the judicial system indicating the appropriate division of revenues. All lease moneys are payable to the Crown. For a surrender to be legal, a band meeting or referendum must be held. A majority of the electors must approve the surrender. If a majority of all eligible electors do not vote at the band meeting, then a second meeting can be held provided a majority of those voting at the first meeting approved the surrender. In the second meeting a majority of the participants voting is sufficient to approve the surrender. The Indian Act makes no provisions for reversing a surrender and restoring land to reserve status.

The allegation of improper surrender of the northwest corner of their reserve forms the basis for another land claim of the Peigan still in the courts. As previously outlined (Chapter 3), departmental policy in the early 1900s was to further land surrenders by Indian bands. Whereas today surrenders are made only for the purpose of leasing land, then surrendered reserve lands were to be sold to white farmers and ranchers. The topic of a land surrender on the Peigan Reserve was first brought up by the Indian agent in May 1909. Though the band told him in June that they did not want to surrender land, he went ahead with plans for a surrender of three to five sections (about eight to thirteen square kilometres) with access to the Canadian Pacific Railway tracks and the Brocket townsite (Rieber 1981: 111). The chiefs objected, and sought the services of a Fort Macleod lawyer. Still determined to obtain a surrender, the agent decided that the band might be more inclined to give up some other portion of its reserve, and so selected forty-five sections (117 square kilometres) in the northeast corner. He forced a vote in July. With their lawyer present, the band members defeated the surrender 46 to 39. The Indian agent pressed a second vote at the end of July. This time it was defeated 60 to 42. Twice defeated in the northeast, the Indian agent then selected a new surrender site in the northwest (Fig. 12). He succeeded in having the band's lawyer barred from observing the vote, received instructions as to price per acre from the Department of the Interior, and had the land surveyed on August 10, 1909. This time he won: The surrender was carried on August 17. Even though the vote was not in accordance with Indian Act stipulations concerning surrenders, even though the agent had obviously brought pressure to bear on the Indians, and despite all protest representations made to Ottawa by the tribe's chief and its lawyer, the federal government did not intervene. The government's neglect did not stop with the surrender. By law, the surrendered lands were to be sold at competitive public auctions. Though auctions were held in 1909, 1910 and 1913, Land Titles Records indicate according to Rieber (1981: 112), that lands were sold in other ways as well. Moreover, rather than being paid by the government for their land directly through purchaser mortgage, the tribe was actually made the mortgagor, in that it was forced to accept time payments from purchasers, many of whom defaulted. This limited the tribe's access to funds for the desired agricultural development. While the Peigan were paid interest on these accounts (with the department taking an administration fee, of course), the actual sale value was reduced since only 4,168 hectar (10,300 acres) of 9,040 hectare (22,338 acres) were actually ever sold. The remaining 4,872 hectar (12,038 acres) were retained by the government from 1909 to 1956 when, at last, they were returned. In the interim, Ottawa had leased those lands to non-Indians. In a final twist to the Peigan surrender, it turned out that Indian improvements to the surrendered land had been valued at $ 2,540 by government surveyors. Instead of increasing the sale price, however, the government sold the lands at unimproved prices and paid the Indian owner out of the unimproved land-sale price. As a result the band was forced to pay the band member for his improvements out of receipts to the band, with the purchaser paying nothing for the improvements. After seventy-one years of frustration, the Peigan finally hired a Calgary law firm to take the case to court. In preparation, the lawyers have not simply put together an oral testimony of band elders. Instead, they have collected every detail of the history of the surrender and prepared a complete economic assessment of earning capacity lost to the Peigan tribe. This multi-million-dollar case is likely to go to trial in the fall.

Another land claim which is not before the courts yet but has been thoroughly researched involves 246 square kilometres (95 square miles) of privately owned prime ranch land immediately south and west of the Peigan Reserve. This claim hinges on a single government document, a December 29, 1882 report from federal surveyor John C. Nelson to the superintendent of Indian Affairs. After describing the location of the main Peigan Reserve the report goes on:

> The grazing reserve adjoining the Piegan Reserve has been surveyed in conformity with the annexed sketch marked (g). The area of this tract is 95 square miles, which also includes the Indian supply farm, known as Pincher Creek Supply Farm. The soil is superior to that of the Piegan Reserve. The herbage is of the richest description, and water abundant in the streams (Indian Affairs Annual Report 1882: 221).

Apparently this tract of land which stretches from the reserve to the Waterton Reservoir was taken back illegally by the federal government and sold to white settlers. Lack of research and adequate documentation caused the matter to go unnoticed until very recently. The place name "Indianfarm Creek" is reminiscent of the land's former use.

Expropriation of reserve land for the construction of Highway No. 3 and secondary road No. 507 (the old Fishburn Trail) are other contentious issues. The question of mineral rights under these lands and the area ceded to the Canadian Pacific Railway was never clarified.

All this "unfinished business" has far-reaching consequences for the development of the reserves. Not only does it directly affect the resource base and financial situation of the bands, but it also has an impact on their general relationship to government departments and thereby may influence decisions concerning not only the reserve communities, but also the wider society. Examples would be the controversy over the eventual construction of a natural gas processing plant on the Morley Reserve (see Chapter 5.4) and the question of where to locate an on-stream storage facility on the Oldman River. In July 1980 a joint ministerial statement was issued on behalf of the Province of Alberta by the Hon. J.W. Cookson, Minister of the Environ-

Figure 12: Peigan Reserve: Areas (recently or presently) subject to dispute

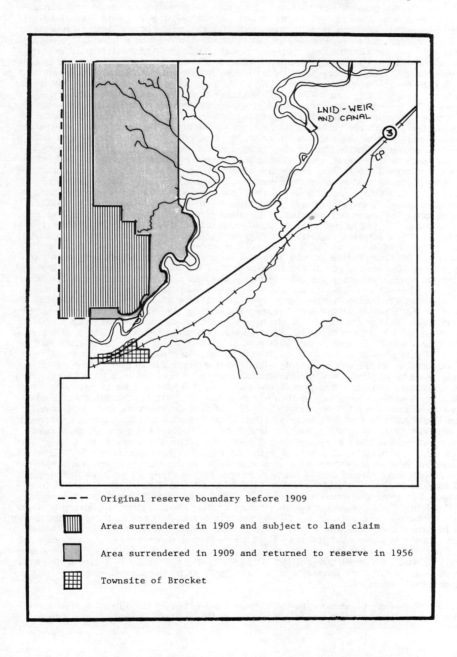

- - - Original reserve boundary before 1909

▧ Area surrendered in 1909 and subject to land claim

▨ Area surrendered in 1909 and returned to reserve in 1956

▦ Townsite of Brocket

Sources: Plan of Part of Peigan No. 147, Range 28, west of 4th M. Prov. of Alberta, surrendered for Sale August 1909. C.N.

ment, and the Hon. Dallas Smith, Minister of Agriculture. The statement indicated that the Alberta government was committed to a long term water resource management in southern Alberta and in particular, additional flow regulation on the Oldman River. This decision is a direct outcome of the major policy declarations made in 1975 with respect to regional water management, the need to rehabilitate existing irrigation systems (hence the struggle over the Oldman River waterbed), and the future irrigation expansion in southern Alberta. These plans include a dam and reservoir on the Oldman River. Several dam sites have been considered, the preferred location being the so-called Three Rivers site (upstream from the Peigan Reserve). However, (very likely due to strong resistance from the ranching community concerned) the provincial government deferred the allocation of funds for the construction of the dam to allow the Peigan the opportunity to study the possibility of locating the dam on the reserve. Its location would be approximately five kilometres (three miles) east of the Brocket townsite. As a result, last year the Peigan set up the "Weasel Valley Water Use Study" to assess the potential impact of the project on the reserve in various areas. The study must be completed prior to fall 1982. Five committees were formed under the chairmanship of councillors to deal with the areas of planning and reseach, environmental impact, social impact, education and economics. The study teams face a monumental task in involving the public in the discussion, and in gathering and spreading the necessary information to enable people to make the crucial decision. If the dam were to be built at the Brocket site, approximately 21,044 hectar (52,000 acres) would be flooded and 2,428 hectar (6,000 acres) would be affected (by dyking, digging back of surrounding river bank etc.). Sixty percent of the land flooded (12,627 hectar or 31,200 acres) would be on the reserve. The river bottom at the potential reservoir site is particularly wide, and the flooded land would constitute 30 per cent of the available river bottom acreage of the reserve. Presently the land is being used as winter pasture for the band's cattle and horses and also as a "summer playground" for the reserve's population. At least sixteen families would have to be moved from their present residences. There is much potential for social disruption during the construction period of five to six years due to the influx of strangers, such as an increase in drug and alcohol abuse, and incidents of racial discrimination. Areas of cultural and archeological significance would be lost and wildlife habitat destroyed. On the other hand the location of this project on the Peigan Reserve would very likely provide a much needed economic boost for the community. Even at this stage the Weasel Valley Water Use Study already employs twenty individuals, many of whom are being trained on the job. During the construction period approximately 250 jobs will be created, and provided preferential hiring and a training program are part of the agreement, much could be achieved for the community in terms of skill development and employment. Care would have to be taken to insure that these benefits are long terms ones, and employment be guaranteed after the dam is built. Moreover a very sizeable cash settlement and/or land exchange would take place, and there would be a long term income for the band in the form of a tax or fee. The economic factor is likely to be a powerful one on a reserve with land and water as its only physical resource and an unemployment rate of 70 per cent. A referendum is going to be held this coming fall for the Peigan to decide whether to give Chief and Council the mandate to negotiate. Whatever the outcome will be, it is likely to be influenced to some degree by the tribe's past experience with land and water deals. After the struggle over the diversion weir on the Oldman River some individuals have little appreciation for the lucrative deal that was finally accomplished because Chief and Council "stuck to their guns"; in their mind the long fight preceding it figures more prominently than the final result, and there may be some reluctance to get involved in any more dealings with the provincial government. On the other hand there is a strong desire in the community to better oneself and to make the best of the limited resource base at the reserve's disposal.

These events illustrate what vital part land plays in the life of Indian communities, be it the settlement of old claims or the accomplishment of new agreements.

5.2.1.2 Land: Quantity and Tenure System

There is an old African proverb: "Men and beasts beget, but land does not beget". In all its simplicity it very well characterizes the land situation on the reserves.

The Treaty Seven Reserves were originally allocated on the basis of one square mile per family of five. Due to the transient character of the population an exact enumeration was a well-nigh impossible task, and population figures in government documents vary considerably. When their reserve was surveyed in 1879, the Stoneys were given 282.3 square kilometres (109 square miles); the number of families was given as seventy-one according to Indian Affairs (Indian Reserve Plans 1889). The first Indian Affairs Annual Report (1881) provides us with a population number of 610. Why and how the Stoneys were never given a fair share of reserve land was already described. The Peigan Reserve, surveyed in 1882, encompassed 475 square kilometres (183.4 square miles) for 193 families, a population of 849. Since then there have been some changes with regard to both reserves.

In 1914 the Rabbit Lake Reserve was transferred to the Stoneys, adding 51,6 square kilometres (20 square miles). In 1945 the Stoneys purchased two ranches adjoining the eastern extremity of the Morley Reserve, comprising about 60 square kilometres (23 square miles). The Eden Valley Reserve was established in 1946 with 18 square kilometres (7 square miles), and Bighorn two years later with 20 square kilometres (8 square miles). Some parcels of land encompassing about 12 square kilometres (4.6 square miles) located north of the Ghost Reservoir were purchased 1959/60. In the land exchange for the Transcanada Highway right-of-way 75 square kilometres (29 square miles) of reserve land were added adjacent to the northern boundary of the Morley Reserve in 1961. Seven years later the widening of the highway resulted in the addition of 44 square kilometres (17 square miles) to the south side of the Morley Reserve plus about 10 square kilometres (4 square miles) to Rabbit Lake. Finally, in the late 1970s, the Stoneys bought the Two Rivers Ranch north of the Ghost Reservoir, comprising 10 square kilometres (3.9 square miles); this land does not yet have reserve status (Fig. 11). This adds up to about 580 square kilometres (224 square miles), without deducting the land lost to reservoir, powerlines and highways, where there are no data available. It means an increase in the Stoney landbase of roughly 100 per cent. At the same time the Stoney population increased by 244 per cent. Due to the possibly illegal surrender the Peigan even experienced a reduction of their reserve lands, while their population grew by 113 per cent. A likely explanation for the striking difference between the Peigan and Stoney population is an inadequate enumeration of the latter due to their continued nomadic lifestyle in the early reserve days. In both cases there now is an obvious discrepancy between a stationary landbase and a rapidly growing population. It is not surprising, therefore, that the population density of both reserves is somewhat higher than that of the provincial census divisions the reserves are part of. The Peigan have a population density of 4.3 per square kilometre compared to 2.7 per square kilometre in census division 3; the Stoneys' (Morley Reserve) population density is 4.1 per square kilometre compared with 3.3 per square kilometre in census division 8 (1976 Census of Canada).

Land-tenure systems can have far-reaching effects on the landuse pattern. As the Red Paper points out (Indian Chiefs of Alberta 1970: 31), "In the culture of Western Canadian Indians, the land is the gift of the Great Spirit, the common legacy of all. The true owners are the children yet unborn. The Indians naturally view their land as a trust with a permanent sign on the corner-post, 'Not for Sale'."

The Indian Act describes reserves as lands "set apart for the use and benefit of a band". Some judicial decisions have held that the band has a real property right in the reserve, a personal and usufructary right to the use and benefit of the land. Another method of describing the band's position is to speak of the Crown holding reserve lands in trust for the band, the band being the beneficiary. Indians are opposed to any system of allotment that would give individuals ownership with rights to sell, but rather want the Indian Act changed to give Indians control of lands without changing the fact that the title is now held in trust. Presently the land holding system on reserve and surrendered lands is characterized by a continuing discretionary power of the Minister. In the past the Department of Indian Affairs made all the decisions as to what land would be used for certain purposes, who used it, how long it was used, and, where applicable, what payment was made for the use of land. Nowadays, on most reserves, including the Peigan and Stoneys, these powers have been transferred to Chief and Council. The band manages its own lands, and negotiations with outside parties are carried out directly by the Band Council. The Indian Act still demands the final approval by the department, but in practice this is a mere formality, and Indian Affairs does not interfere with the substance of agreements.

When the reserves were first established, the plains tribes had no concept of individual use and ownership of land (1). Initial sedentary settlement tended to be in "villages", often corresponding to the traditional bands within the tribes. Equally, farming was attempted on a communal basis. But the government's goal was for Indian society to be atomized. Thus, the government would deal with individuals rather than with bands. Their desire for atomization extended to breaking up the villages in the reserves, and to put an end to communal farming and ranching. The Indian was to be taught to be an individual farmer or cattle raiser on his own piece of land. Consequently, reserves were increasingly subdivided into small plots, and individuals were given their own parcel of land to work. Generally legal security of possession of the right to use a portion of reserve land is only obtained by a band member if there is an allotment of the land by the band council with the approval of the Minister. The documentary proof of this right is either a Location Ticket (2) (if issued before the coming into effect of the current Indian Act in 1951) or a Certificate of Possession (under the current legislation). The right can be expropriated for band or Indian Affairs purposes. It terminates if the band surrenders the land. The land can also be leased for the benefit of the holder, without being surrendered. Landuse rights can pass by devise, or can be transferred to the band or to another band member by the Indian holding these rights; no transfer of land is effective though, until it is approved by the Minister.

Many bands, particularly on the prairies, and including the Peigan and Stoneys, choose not to use Certificates of Possession or any of the Indian Act provisions for internal Indian land holding on reserves. They adhere to what may be called "customary" or "traditional" land allotment patterns, in contrast with those found in the Indian Act. These bands allot land to individual band members, but

---

1) For an interesting comparison of property concepts in European and Indian society see Leroy Little Bear's testimony at a hearing of the Berger Commission in Toronto (O'Malley 1976: 238-243).
2) The Location Ticket was an innovation of the original Indian Act (1876). The government regarded it as an essential feature of the "civilization" process and a necessity for enfranchisement. It was a means by which the Indian could demonstrate that he had adopted the European concept of private property, which was an additional test of whether he had become "civilized". The Superintendent General had the reserve surveyed into individual lots, which the band council could assign to individual band members. As a form of title the Superintendent General would then give the band member a Location Ticket. But before a ticket was issued, the individual had to prove that he was "civilized" (according to earlier legislation: literate in either English or French, free of debt, and of good moral character - standards that few of the colonists would have been able to meet!). On passing this first test, and receiving a Location Ticket, the Indian entered a three year probationary period during which he had to demonstrate that he would use the land as a Euro-Canadian might. If he passed these tests, he was enfranchised and given title to his land. Thus the land became part of the surrounding municipality. This process was mostly designed for and was most effective with the Indians east of Lake Superior, who were considered more advanced. Marie Marule (Kainai News Oct. No. 2, 1981) points out that the Location Tickets/Certificates of Possession resulted in serious problems on various eastern reserves. Enterprising individuals would buy off other people's certificates and then disproportionately control the band's landbase; 10 per cent of a community might control 50 per cent of the land.

do so at the discretion of the band council. They avoid any Ministerial validation of the allotment. The allottee, on the other hand, has no more legal security of tenure than the band council is prepared to permit. The practice of this land policy and the problems encountered slightly vary from reserve to reserve.

On the Peigan Reserve 244 square kilometres (94 square miles) or 57 per cent of the reserve's landbase has been individually allotted (Fig. 13). Much of today's distribution pattern goes back to the 1920s, when the Peigan population numbered around 500. The educational policy of this period (industrial schools) placed particular emphasis on manual training and agricultural instruction, and band members interested in agriculture and prepared to break land were allocated a parcel of land by the Indian Agent. Yet, the relapse small-scale agriculture experienced after World War I (see Chapter 3) was to repeat itself in the 1950s, when mechanization and related changes intensified, and farming in the old way became just too uneconomical. Many of the older individuals on the reserve interviewed during the survey recalled working their land with a horse-drawn plough until the late 1950s. Then they resorted to leasing their plots to non-Indian farmers and ranchers because they saw no other way of making a living. While reserve land had been leased before, it was only at this point in time that band members turned to leasing out their small individual plots to off-reserve enterprises. In 1966 when liquor was first admitted onto Indian reserves, individual land was transferred rapidly and cheaply with some individuals amassing large acreages in the process. At the same time, with the onset of self-government, political factors gained importance in the process of land allocation.

Today there are about 200 "landowners" (this somewhat incorrect term is chosen for convenience) on the Peigan Reserve. Among these 160 have rights to arable land, 78 to grazing land; around 60 per cent own both categories. The average size of a large holding is 390 hectar (960 acres), while small holdings average 65 hectar (160 acres). Small plots account for 75 per cent of all individual land holdings. Sixty per cent of the individually allocated grazing land is being leased out, and 90 per cent of the arable land. This becomes understandable after another look at the land-people ratio. Assuming that the reserve land was to be farmed by an Indian farmer, Price and Associates Limited (1967) estimate that this individual would require a 485 hectar (1,200 acres) unit in order to meet the following conditions:
a) Pay one-quarter share of return to band for the use of their resource
b) Pay for required machinery
c) Provide a reasonable standard of living for the operator and his family.

With regard to ranching the same source estimates that a satisfactory living could be made on a pasture capacity of 115 animal units. Assuming a general carrying capacity of 10.1 hectar (25 acres) per animal unit per year (see Chapter 5.3.1) this would amount to 1,162 hectar (2,875 acres) per ranch. Even if this acreage would be reduced by the use of a six months grazing system, supplementary feed and use of the community pasture, the discrepancy between the actual holdings and economic units is still evident. With regard to both farming and ranching not even the large holdings on the reserve which constitute only a small percentage of the individual plots reach minimum economic unit size. The result of this distribution pattern is the exorbitant leasing out of valuable land with two-thirds of the revenue leaving the reserve and only one-third being paid to the "owner". There being only one Peigan farmer, almost all of the reserve's arable land is farmed by non-band members on a share-cropping basis, and a sizeable portion of the reserve's pasture is being grazed by off-reserve cattle (Fig. 14 and 15). During the author's survey it was found that 66 per cent of the landowners interviewed (twenty-one out of thirty-two) leased their land; of these only two leased it to fellow band members. Among these "armchair farmers" all economic strata are represented: councillors, office clerks, labourers, busdrivers, disabled persons, welfare recipients to name but a few. While a few individuals argue that they are just not interested in either farming or ranching, the majority expresses considerable inclination to go into full-time ranching if more land and capital were available. But the way things are, the leasing of land seems to be a legal and socially acceptable way ot contributing to one's living on the Peigan Reserve. If there is a degree of resentment among the landless (which is likely), it does not manifest itself in the same way as on the

Figure 13: Peigan Reserve: Land Tenure

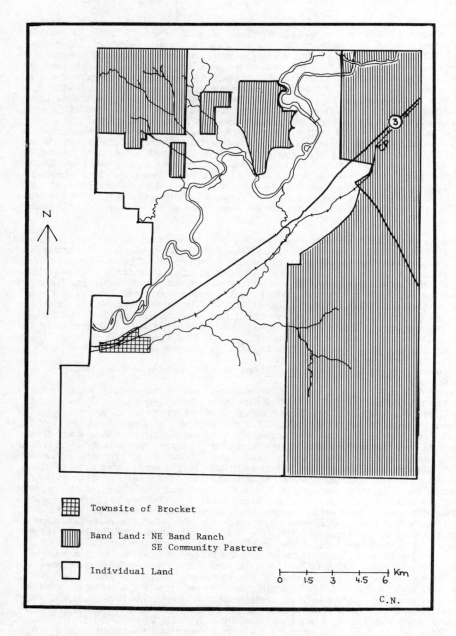

Sources: Peigan Tribal Administration

Figure 14: Peigan Reserve: Leased Land

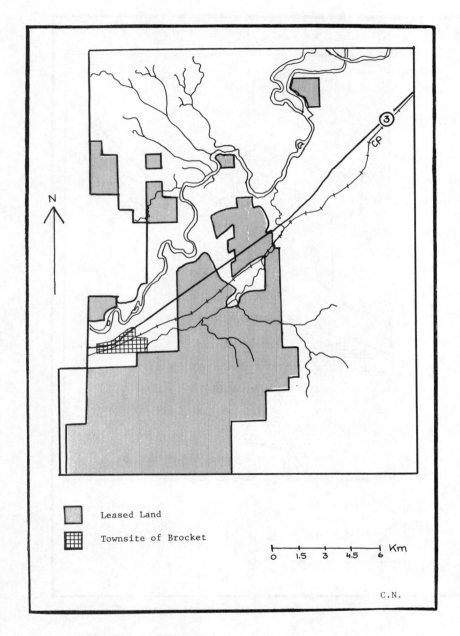

Sources: Peigan Tribal Administration

Figure 15: Peigan Reserve: Land under Cultivation (1980)

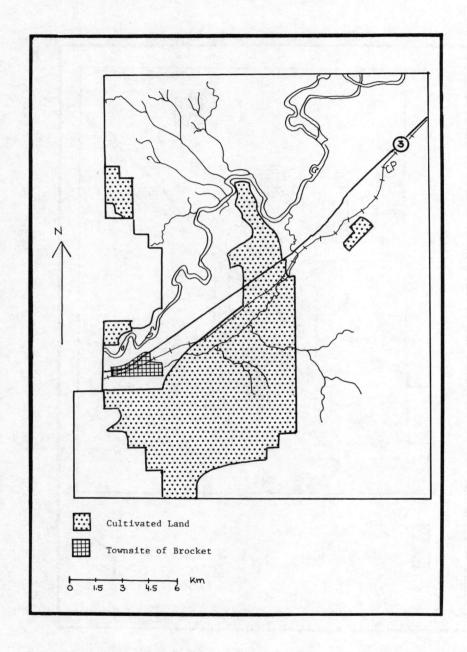

Sources: After Photomap compiled from 1980 vertical aerial photographs Roll No. A25569. Energy, Mines and Resources Canada 1981

neighbouring Blood Reserve, where a landless band member demonstratively erected his teepee beside the band's administration building last October, and where political pressure groups try to force the tribal council to set up a workable land policy. The land question is at present the most controversial and emotional subject on that reserve. On the Peigan Reserve, in order to lease their land, individuals must apply to the band council, who in turn negotiates the matter with the Department of Indian Affairs; the final agreement is signed by the permittee and Indian Affairs. The land is usually leased for a period of three years. The band retains jurisdiction over the way the leased land is being used, with regard to stocking rates, farming techniques etc. There was, for example, a severe winderosion problem in 1981, and the Peigan Lands Department implemented zero-till farming (no summerfallow) on their leased land. Peigan landowners have no obligation to the band for the usage of farming or grazing land. Before 1966 ranchers had to pay $ 6 into a "ranch account" for every head of cattle and every horse they grazed; and equally until 1979 farmland owners had to pay 20 per cent of their return to the band. There is no definite land policy on the Peigan Reserve; the council handles disputes over land individually. The main source of contention apparently is the question of inheritance. Normally this matter is decided within the family, and the parcel of land is transferred to the surviving spouse or handed down to one child. But increasingly people appeal to council to settle arising disputes; and in some cases the land returns to the band to be transferred to a new applicant. There is the possibility (and tentative plan for the future) of subdividing and allocating part of the communally managed grazing land.

Individual land tenure on the Stoney Reserve is subject to the same customary system. Here, however, it is even more flexible and informal. The division between "landowners" and landless band members is less pronounced than on the Blackfoot Reserves, as every family by custom has the right to fence off or use a parcel of land to graze some livestock. There are "acceptable" limits as to the size of holdings an individual may fence off for himself, the majority measuring under 65 hectar (160 acres). Sixty-nine per cent of the Chiniki sample claimed a parcel of land, with the majority being uncertain about its exact size. Only two out of those twenty-two landowners utilized larger areas, in the neighbourhood of 260 hectar (640 acres). There is no land registry and as a result there are no data regarding the number of landowners or size of holdings. At the same time no land has been formally designated as bandland (except the STAR-Ranch); although some unsettled areas have a tradition of communal use (Fig. 16), theoretically individuals are allowed to take their share of this land. About 60 per cent of the main Morley Reserve have been taken up individually. Naturally certain holdings came to be associated with certain families, and the land distribution pattern goes back a long time in history. There being well over 400 households on the Morley Reserve and its physical features imposing limitations on settlement and utilization of some parts, there is a pronounced land shortage. The individual holdings are uneconomically small, especially in view of the fact that the wooded character of a major part of the reserve necessitates even larger ranch units to make a living than the Peigan Reserve. Nevertheless all the individually used land is utilized for grazing livestock. and none is leased to non-band members. Although leasing was practised before self-government, it was discontinued about a decade ago as a matter of policy, and thanks to their gas royalties band members do not depend on this source of income. Use of reserve land is free for the Stoneys. There is no defined land policy; disputes arising over questions of inheritance or transactions are handled by council individually.

Thus the land situation on the reserves is characterized by a peculiar tension caused by the combination of hard economic facts, perceived and/or real political favouritism and the enduring Indian wholistic concept of land ownership. Pointing towards supposed communal ownership of the landbase, the landless feel justified to ask where their profit from this resource is likely to occur. Due to the population increase and historically established distribution patterns only a limited number of families can reap the major benefits. Sober economics - as they govern Western society - would even call for a complete re-allotment process in order to create economic ranching and farming units. It is obvious that this is totally unrealistic. An editorial in Kainai News (Feb. No. 2, 1982) tackling this problem, suggests that if all band members could reach consensus that all landholders must work their own

Figure 16: Morley Reserve: Land Tenure

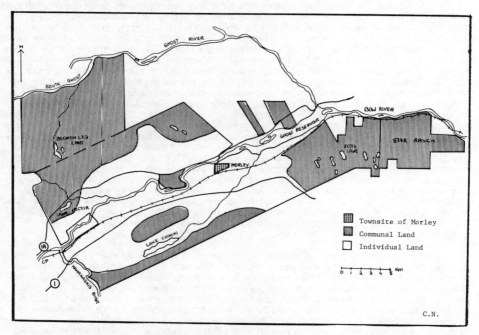

Sources: Stoney Tribal Administration

land, then an acreage payment could be poured into the band capital account and benefit all band members. The farmers/ranchers would get a percentage, and the landless would receive a percentage. The acreage payment could be invested in a high interest account which in the future could enable the tribe to buy more land off the reserve. But whatever solution will finally be attempted, the implementation of any land policy will infringe upon long established individual rights, and many problems will have to be overcome.

5.2.2 The People

5.2.2.1 Demography

Considering that only 13 per cent of all the Indian bands in Canada have a membership in excess of one thousand people, the Peigan and the Stoneys definitely belong to the larger bands in the country with populations of 1,812 and 2,296 (Chiniki 736, Wesley 747, Bearspaw 813) respectively. Both bands (1), however, had experienced a radical decline in their numbers earlier this century. The Peigan started off their reserve life with a population around 900 in the 1880s. The last figure given by the Indian Affairs Annual Reports (before only districts were reported) was 424 in 1915. The population continued to decline to a low ebb of about

---

1) The Canadian usage of the terms "tribe" and "band" is interchangeable. More correctly, however, we would have to say, that the Stoney Tribe consists of three bands - Chiniki, Wesley and Bearspaw - who have a limited degree of political autonomy and their own chiefs and councillors, while the Peigan Tribe comprises six recognized bands who have mainly cultural significance (for example in the transfer of ceremonial bundles).

250 following the disastrous influenza epidemic in 1918. From then on a gradual population increase started until the late 1940s when the population growth became more rapid. By the late 1950s the Peigan had regained their former numbers of around 900. Since then their population has doubled.

The Stoneys' population was equally ravaged by disease during their early reserve days, but reliable population estimates are virtually non-existent. Probably due to the greater degree of mobility of the Stoney people early Indian Affairs population data show a great deal of inconsistency, such as a population of 566 for 1891, 449 for 1892, and 647 for 1893. The last figure given by the Indian Affairs Annual Reports was 654 in 1915. Like the Peigan the Stoneys experienced a rapid population growth since the late 1940s, resulting in their present population of over two thousand (1).

The population characteristics of the Peigan and Stoneys are typical for the second stage of the demographic transition model, where the birth rate, although declining, is still significantly higher than the mortality rate. As there are no detailed data available for the two reserves, some trends for the provincial Treaty Indian population shall be shown instead, based on Siggner and Locatelli (1980). In recent years there has been a marked decline in the birth rate of the Indian population. In 1967 the birth rate among Indians was 46.8 births per 1,000 population which was more than double the birth rate of the total provincial population. By 1976 the Indian rate had declined to 33.1 births per 1,000 population, a 29 per cent drop, whereas the overall provincial birth rate had only decreased by 14 per cent to 18.0 births per 1,000 population. An important aspect of this phenomenon is that while the number of births among Indians has declined, the number of females in the childbearing years (aged 15-49) has increased from about 4,943 to 7,748 between 1966 and 1976. It seems likely that the decline in the number of births will continue despite the fact that the number of women entering the childbearing years is still expected to increase during this decade. This is due to the Indian "baby-boom" becoming effective. Both the Indian and the non-Indian population of Canada have experienced a "baby-boom" in the second half of the twentieth century, although the Indian boom lagged behind the non-Indian one by several years and peaked in the mid-sixties.

The Indian mortality rate has also been greatly reduced in recent years, although this rate is still considerably higher than that of the provincial population of Alberta. The Indian infant mortality rate has declined from 56.9 infant deaths per 1,000 live births in 1963 to 25.5 deaths per 1,000 live births in 1976. The provincial rate was 19.9 in 1963 down to 11.4 in 1976. There are substantial differences in the death rates by certain age groups between the Indian and the white population of the province. The greatest differences are found between the ages of 15 and 49, where the Indian death rates are at least four times higher than the provincial rates. For instance, in the 20-29 age group the Indian death rate is 7.8 per 1,000 population while the provincial rate is only 1.4; and in the 30-39 age group the Indian rate of 10.4 is seven times greater than the non-Indian rate of 1.5. As to the cause of death, accidents, poisonings and violence are responsible for over 36 per cent of all Indian deaths compared to less than 13 per cent of all such deaths in the provincial population. The next major cause of death among Indians stems from diseases of the circulatory system which account for 17 per cent, followed by diseases of the respiratory system (8 per cent), neoplasms or cancer (6 per cent) and diseases of the digestive system (5 per cent). Major causes of accidental deaths among Albertan Indians during the 1974-1976 period were motor vehicle and train accidents (38 per cent), firearms (14 per cent) und drowning (10 per cent). Many of these deaths are suicidal. Especially the former two are very much in evidence on the Stoney and Peigan Reserves.

---

1) Significantly, only a few decades ago, one assumed that the Indian would not even survive as a race: "Doubtless all the tribes will disappear" (Jenness 1932: 264).

The population pyramids depicting the age and sex structure of the Peigan and Stoney samples (1) (Fig. 17) show clearly that we are dealing with young populations. The broad base and narrow apex indicate a high birth rate and comparatively short lifespan and corresponding high death rate. The Stoneys and the Peigan are burdened with a high dependency ratio - the number of dependents (under age 15 and age 65 and over) per 100 people in the labour force age group (15-64) - compared to Canada as a whole. About 40 per cent of the Stoney and Peigan populations is under the age of 15 compared to about one-third of the overall population. Approximately 60 per cent are younger than 25. But the dependent population 15 years of age and younger has undergone a marked change as a percentage of the total population. Whereas, for example in 1966 this group represented 48.5 per cent of the Stoney population (Underwood, McLellan and Associates Limited 1969) its share has declined to 39.1 per cent of the sample in 1981. As the same time the young adult age group 15-29 has grown considerably in proportion. This relative change again is caused by the maturing of the 1960s "baby-boom". As a consequence there seems to be a gradual shift towards the third stage (late expanding stage) of the demographic transition, where the rate of expansion slows down.

There is a fairly even distribution of males and females in the young and middle ages. A large imbalance exists, however, in the numbers of males and females over 55. There are considerably fewer women than men, a reverse situation to that for Canada. This situation probably reflects the harsh conditions often endured by women on the reserves, strenuous labour and frequent child bearing.

An important implication of the decline in the birth rate is that the family size will also decline. At present, the shape of the population pyramids shows quite clearly that Indian families on both reserves are substantially larger than non-Indian families. In the following we must distinguish, however, between household and (nuclear as opposed to extended) family. The term "family" refers to husband and wife, either childless or living with non-married children, or one parent living with never married children. A household is all persons living in one dwelling, whether they belong to one family or several families. These definitions conform to those of the Census of Canada.

During the survey on the Peigan Reserve it was found that 43.1 per cent of the sampled households encompassed more than one family. 34.5 per cent actually contained two families, very often consisting of the elderly parents and their unmarried children plus a married child with spouse and offspring(s). Frequently the second family consists of an unwed daughter with children or just a young couple. 8.6 per cent of the households had additional individuals (always kin) living with the nuclear family, like a brother or sister, an old parent, or a young nephew, cousin or grandchild as informally adopted wards. On one occasion there was a foster child in a family. On the Stoney Reserve the situation was fairly similar, with 40.6 per cent of the sampled households consisting of more than one nuclear family, 31.3 per cent combined two families, while 9.3 per cent had additional kin living with the household head's family. The average household size on the Peigan Reserve was five persons, on the Stoney Reserve 5.2. Those Peigan households with just one family averaged 3.9 family members; only 15 per cent thereof had more than three children. With the Stoney sample the difference was less pronounced: The average family size of the one family households was 4.8; 37 per

---

1) Population pyramids were constructed for the Stoney and Peigan samples, because no tribal data were available. While they do depict the general population characteristics, the strong variations among single age- or sex-groups are not representative. The following data were available for the Peigan Tribe (1979):

Age	Male	Female	Total	Per cent
0-16	412	434	846	48.3
17-25	185	171	356	20.3
26-35	121	128	249	14.2
36-45	63	65	128	7.3
46-55	45	49	94	5.4
over 55	43	34	77	4.4
	869	881	1,750	100.0

Figure 17: Population Pyramids for the Peigan and Stoney Samples

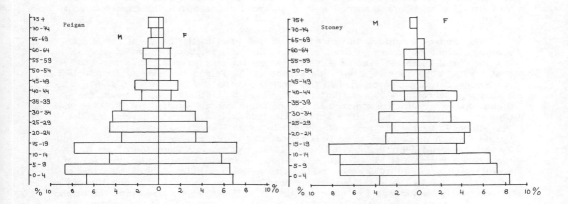

cent of these had more than three children. The high percentage of households including more than one family is probably best explained as a culturally conditioned - the attitude "We take each other in" - response to an economic dilemma, the persistent housing shortage (see Chapter 6). Besides, a heritage of the "extended family" notion, it is not uncommon for young people to stay with older relatives in response to family emergencies or parents' employment.

As mentioned previously, the amount of absenteism is not very great on either reserve. In the 1970s the proportion of Indians living off-reserve was 6 per cent for the Peigan and only 2 per cent for the Stoneys, lower than for the other three Treaty Seven Reserves. This appears to be more a matter of cultural preference (and due to a feeling of security on the reserve) than a reflection of economic opportunities, as the Stoneys have always been characterized by a very small number of migrants, even before the creation of on-reserve employment, and the Peigan find themselves in a similar situation as the Blood and Northern Blackfoot in terms of on-reserve employment and proximity of off-reserve centres.

In conclusion we can say that the two most important demographic facts for the Stoneys and Peigan are that

a) they are still characterized by a young population with a high dependency ratio, and
b) their labour force now experiences the full brunt of the Indian baby boom.

The latter also has an impact on the requirements of secondary and post-secondary education.

5.2.2.2 Education

Havighurst (1972: 92) presents meaning and situation of Indian education in a nutshell: "Education is always a process of teaching a culture, and the education provided by the whites for the Indians has always been aimed at teaching the white culture, or at least some element of it, to people who have been reared in another culture."

Whether we look at the "Paternalistic Ideology" phase of federal and provincial government policy on Indian education before 1945 (to which older community members were subjected) or at the "Democratic Ideology" phase afterwards (1945 to the present) (Frideres 1974: 32) which enabled natives to attend school off the reserve, schooling has always been and to a very considerable degree still is characterized by cultural alienation and a total lack of control Indians have over their own education.

For most of a century Indian education had been in the hands of the missionaries and other employees of the Christian churches, whose attitudes of paternalism and moral rectitude exacted a heavy toll on Indian students. Thus the Anglicans started a school and a boarding school on the Peigan Reserve in the late 1880s; the Roman Catholic Church opened the first school on the reserve in 1887 and added a boarding school in 1896. The latter only closed in 1961. The situation on the Stoney Reserve was characterized by the constant control exerted by the Methodist Church and later by the United Church (in 1925, the Methodist Church, the Congregational Church and groups of the Presbyterian Church formed together as the United Church of Canada). The first school on the reserve was an orphanage built by the Reverend John McDougall in 1874-1875; a day school developed from it. In the 1880s a residential school was established, in which the students lived for ten months each year. In 1925 a new residential school was built which ceased functioning as such in the mid-1950s, when more and more students attended the day school, newly established by Indian Affairs in 1945. Generally speaking, the emphasis in all these church-controlled schools was to give the children a Christian education which would prepare a girl to be a good housewife and a boy to be a good farmer. To keep down the costs of running the schools, children were assigned numerous tasks in the schools, residences and school farms. Rigid regulations - including the non-use of their native tongue - had to be obeyed and were frequently enforced by whippings. Many former students of these schools on both reserves perceive that hard physical work figured more prominently than any kind of academic training. With many teachers being non-certified - religious fervor being a more important factor in their appointment - education on the reserves did not even come close to measuring up to the standards of white schools. The overriding goal was segregating the children from their parents and kin and alienating them from their culture. Indian culture was condemned explicitly and implicitly. As John Snow (1977: 110) remembers from his own experience in the United Church Residential School, his classes consisted of teachings in Protestant religion and ethics, the three R's, and European and Church history. From listening to these teachings it would seem to the children that the only good people on earth were non-Indians and specifically white Christians. Everything that they had been brought up to believe in - the faith of their fathers, the knowledge of their medicine men and women - were presented to them as false and works of the Devil (ibid.). The social disruption of the educational system and the cultural irrelevancy to their everyday-life naturally resulted in an astronomically high drop-out rate, not to mention what such treatment does to a people's self-esteem. Education beyond grade eight was not encouraged. At least on the Stoney Reserve, in fact the school really only went through grade six, with very few pupils staying the extra two years. In theory, secondary education was available in regular schools in nearby towns. In practice, however, poor preparation, difficulties of transportation and the overall discouraging attitude of non-Indian officialdom made continuing education all but unavailable to young Indians (1).

In the 1960s Indian Affairs took over the control of reserve schools from the churches. By this time, too, the federal government's school integration policy was in full swing. The department's theory behind this policy was that the sooner the Indian left the reserve and moved into Canadian society-at-large, the better it would be for him, and the sooner his overall integration would be achieved. Thus the general goal was still the same as before, only the churches had tried to reach it by

---

1) For some far-reaching socio-economic implications of the churches' control of Indian education, especially in the case of Roman Catholicism, see Frideres, J.S., ed., 1974, <u>Canada's Indians. Contemporary Conflicts</u>, Scarborough, pp. 33 ff.

"education in isolation". Although the new policy had been initiated in 1945, it was only in the 1960s that Indian parents in growing numbers forsook the on-reserve federal day-schools and enrolled their children next to non-Indians in the schools in nearby off-reserve communities. To promote its policy the department resorted to various means, on the reserves as well as in the white communities. Special clothing allowances issued only to children attending off-reserve schools were to entice parents to let their children leave the reserves. On the other hand the provincial schools would not only receive per capita grants from Indian Affairs for each Indian enrollee, but sometimes even substantial sums for additional facilities taken from capital expenditure money allocated to the reserve schools. Children who cannot commute on a daily basis are accommodated in white foster homes, the foster parents being paid by the department to provide for the students. By the late 1960s and early 1970s a large number of young Indians had switched to non-federal (= off-reserve) schools, mainly due to decreasing funds for the federal reserve schools and the non-availability of secondary education. In 1966 68.8 per cent of the Peigan students attended integrated provincial schools, and a considerably lower percentage of Stoney students, roughly 30 per cent (Bob White, Indian Affairs, personal communication). Many of the children attended the federal schools until grade six and then transferred for secondary education. This switch from one school-system to another has serious disruptive influence on the educational and social development of native children, the change of social milieu and discrimination being the major disruptive factors. Frideres (1974: 35) points out that living on the reserve, Indian students would already have been subjected to institutionalized discrimination without being immediately and directly aware of it. But moving to an integrated school means daily exposure to direct discrimination. Their self-concepts can be seriously and permanently distorted. The short-term effect of discrimination can be reflected in lower marks and eventually it can lead to dropping out. Other problems, such as lack of input in the decision-making processes, alienating curricula and cultural irrelevancy already encountered during the "missionary period" were only perpetuated under this new policy. Consequently, as Indians became more and more aware of the problems of attending integrated schools, the trend of native enrollment started to reverse itself around 1976. Even though, on the Peigan Reserve, in 1979, the percentage of students attending the Peigan School in Brocket was still relatively low with 36.7 per cent, which is probably due to the proximity of Fort Macleod and Pincher Creek - within bussing range - and to the persistant lack of facilities and qualified staff in the reserve school. On the Morley Reserve only approximately 100 or 14 per cent of the roughly 700 students attend provincial schools, the vast majority in Exshaw and a negligible number in Springbank and Cochrane. On the Bighorn and Eden Valley Reserves all children attend federal reserve schools.

The social incoherence of the educational system throughout the decades, its lack of quality and its imposition by one culture on another is clearly reflected in the Stoneys' and Peigan's educational achievement. The average highest school grade completed by the household heads (of all ages) of the sample on the Stoney Reserve is 6.7, in the Peigan sample it is 8.2. The discrepancy in educational standards between Indians and their white counterparts decreases with age, but it increases the higher we move up the educational ladder. There is a slight indication that the church-controlled reserve schools provided a higher-grade education on the Peigan Reserve than the United Church did for the Stoneys and/or that attendance was more strictly enforced by the RCMP among the Peigan than with the Stoneys, as there are more members of the older generation (over 50) among the Stoneys with no schooling at all or only up to grade six. Among the middle-aged and younger people a grade eight or grade nine education is fairly common on both reserves. Six individuals interviewed on the Peigan Reserve (10 per cent, which is likely to be a overrepresentation in the sample) graduated from high school; of these four attended college. Two members of the Chiniki interviewed (6 per cent) finished grade twelve; one attended the university, the other went to Mount Royal College.

Looking at the 1979 enrollment of Peigan students at the various grade levels (on and off reserve), it becomes clear that there is no longer the strong concentration of pupils in the lower elementary grades, which characterized the situation in the 1960s. The distribution is fairly even from grade one to grade ten, averaging 9.1 per cent of the students in each grade (ranging from a maximum of 11.1 per cent in grade one to a minimum of 6.7 per cent in grade six). The sudden drop-off occurs at the senior-high level, with only 4.1 per cent of the students enrolled in grade eleven and 5.1 per cent in grade twelve. As can be expected, the participation of native students in post-secondary education is very low. Almost 21 per cent of young Peigan Indians between the ages of 13 and 18 are out of school, and unskilled and unemployed. The dismal educational and employment situation of Peigan youth is particularly reflected by the age group between 19 and 25. Almost 70 per cent are unskilled and unemployed; 19 per cent are both skilled and gainfully employed; and a mere 11 per cent of this group are still undergoing some kind of schooling.

The situation does not seem to be too different with the Stoneys. Although no detailed statistics are available, there appears to be a gradual tapering off in the number of students after grade six, whereas only a very low percentage of students attend senior high school (Bob White, Indian Affairs, personal communication). Five or six Stoneys attend university full-time.

Thus it is fairly evident that - although there has been marked progress during the last two decades - the Peigan and Stoneys still have a long way to go to catch up educationally with the non-Indian population (1). The most feasible way to do this is by "Indian Control of Indian Education". This was the title of a document drawn up by the National Indian Brotherhood in 1972 and accepted in principle by the Minister of Indian Affairs shortly after. Although the theoretical endorsement of this policy was a far cry from its actual realization, especially where the question of funding is concerned (Cardinal 1977: 56 ff), there have been some pronounced changes since the mid-1970s. More effort has been put into the improvement of the reserve schools, and more native teachers and teacher's aides have been placed there. Some interesting developments have taken place especially on the postsecondary level.

There are three schools on the Morley Reserve today: a kindergarten, an elementary school and a junior high school extending to grade ten. These schools are under the jurisdiction of the Department of Indian Affairs and Northern Development. There is an all-Stoney education committee with advisory and informative function and limited curriculum input, but the administration of the schools, including the hiring of staff is a federal responsibility. The Stoneys have devised quite a unique education program of their own, the Stoney Cultural Education Program (SCEP). The SCEP was formed in 1972 by a merger of the Stoney Language Program and the Oral History Program under the auspices of the Tribal Education Committee. It was a reaction to the realization of the degrading effect of white textbooks, especially in social sciences, and of the problems encountered by native children in an alien learning environment. Whereas the Language Program was concerned with the development of an alphabet for the Stoney language, the Oral History Program was an interview-type project focussing on the interrogation of elders. Fieldworkers would tape interviews on a variety of topics, such as religion, medicine, history, philosophy, land disputes etc. Finally the material was translated into English, written down in both languages and compiled into booklet form (in the band-owned printshop) for use in the school. Moreover, as Harbeck (1973) points out, when describing SCEP, one of the program's major goals is not just teaching about the Stoney way, but a reorientation of the entire curriculum around the Stoney way. A first step in this direction is taking into account that the Stoney child enters into formal education with quite different pre-school experiences from the non-Stoney child, i.e. with a native fluency in the Stoney language and some familiarity with the essentials of Stoney culture. As a result English should be taught from a second-language point of view rather than in a first language method as has

---

1) A study of school programs for Alberta native students has been initiated by the Curriculum Policies Board, Alberta Department of Education. It will investigate successful and unsuccessful programs in schools located on and off reserves, in order to find ways to improve Indian students' performance in public integrated schools. Its final report was expected by June 1982.

been done traditionally. SCEP is trying to design and implement a curriculum which will achieve the same high academic objectives underlying the Alberta curriculum while taking into account the differences in world view and experiences of both cultures. SCEP staff are employed as teacher's aides in order to familiarize themselves with the problems encountered in the classroom and to produce the needed teaching materials in cooperation with the regular (Indian Affairs employed) teachers. Others attend the University of Calgary or the Southern Alberta Institute of Technology in order to acquire teaching, research or secretarial skills as required by the program.

The Peigan School in Brocket extends to grade nine. It was founded in the early 1960s after the Roman Catholic boarding school had closed down. A Peigan school board is headed by a tribal council member, but has - with one of its members sitting on the selection committee - only advisory function in the hiring and firing of teaching staff and virtually no input in curriculum design, the school being operated by the federal government. Only one of the eight teachers is a Peigan Indian. Nevertheless, an effort is also being made here, to incorporate Blackfoot culture into the teaching, although there is no comprehensive program similar to SCEP. Moreover, the language situation is somewhat different on this reserve compared to the Stoney Reserves.

Among the Stoneys the Stoney language, a Sioux dialect, is not only mastered but commonly used by all generations. That is not to say that there is no communication gap between the older and younger generations. Meanings and terminology vary; changes in pronunciation and syntax develop into communication problems. The emotional reaction to all this has a greater negative effect on communication than the change itself. Therefore, a great need is seen by the Stoneys not only to have the young generation study the older generation's language, but to educate the community to the nature of language change which is a natural process in any living language. In the sample interviewed it was found that 47 per cent of the households - containing all age groups - use Stoney as their only language at home, whereas the remaining 53 per cent use English as well as Stoney. Only 1.6 per cent (two individuals in their thirties and forties) of the household heads said of themselves that they were not fluent in the Stoney language. The picture presenting itself on the Peigan Reserve is a bit different. Here only 17.2 per cent of the households visited use Blackfoot as their exclusive means of communication; 80 per cent of the heads of these households are older than forty years. 41.4 per cent of the households use Blackfoot as well as English; there is no predominant age group in this category. The same percentage (41.4) speak only English at home; here younger household heads under the age of forty predominate with 71 per cent. 19 per cent of the household heads interviewed claimed to be not fluent in Blackfoot, here again the younger generation is represented with 91 per cent. Many of the younger Peigan in their twenties and thirties understand their native language quite well, but have difficulty speaking it. Generational differences in the spoken language occur here as well. Generally, Peigan children can be expected to be more familiar with the English language than Stoney children, although they do encounter language problems at school. In fact, Blackfoot classes are being taught at the Peigan School, in order to revive the language among the young generation. Besides, while the provincial curriculum is followed by the Peigan School, the Oldman River Cultural Centre in Brocket furnishes resource material to be used for instruction.

Efforts to provide a culturally integrated education are not confined to the reserve communities. Catering mainly to native people in southern Alberta, the Plains Indian Cultural Survival School (PICSS) in Calgary, founded in 1979, is a striking example of Indian selfhelp. Housed in the basement of Vincent Massey Junior High School, the school provides academic courses combined with a cultural program, where students learn Indian skills, language and culture. Enrollment was 107 in 1980, up from 57 students enrolled during the school's first year. It teaches grades seven to twelve. Before its establishment no other alternatives were available for Indian students who could not fit into the integrated public schools. In 1980, 85 per cent of the PICSS students were either former dropouts or irregular school attenders. Elders are involved in the programs, and the board members of the PICSS Society are all Indian. Parents are encouraged to get involved and they have a say in the programs. In 1980, there were four non-native teachers in the academic program, whereas all the teachers in the cultural courses were native; an Indian cultural director works with all the teachers. The school's academic programs are funded by the Calgary Board of Education, but the cultural school depends on private and corporate donations.

In the field of post-secondary education it was already noted that a large percentage is involved in "vocational training" and general "upgrading" courses. Vocational training includes programs in carpentry, sheetmetal work, motor mechanics and farming. Upgrading can be viewed as a "catch all" category, and is offered by Indian Affairs as well as by some colleges like the Lethbridge Community College, catering mainly to the Peigan and Blood. The Stoneys receive an Indian Affairs grant for adult education, which is administered under local control and also used for this purpose. Upgrading classes are geared towards natives who have prematurely dropped out of school and are interested in improving their level of education, and also towards mature adults seeking employment but lacking the necessary academic skills in reading, writing and simple mathematics. The Lethbridge Community College courses are sixteen weeks long with five hours instruction per day. Outreach workers on the individual reserves help with information diffusion and assist interested applicants.

Although native student enrollment in colleges and universities has increased phenomenally over the last couple of years, there still are many inadequacies to be overcome. The Lethbridge Community College (using Peigan and Blood interviewers) conducted a five year survey among native students who attended the college between 1977 and 1981. Its main purpose was to determine the reasons for the high native student dropout rate, which has been a persistant problem for many years. The reasons discovered were not new: reluctance of landlords to rent to native people, long drives from both the Peigan and Blood reserves to the college and students being unprepared academically and culturally were the general obstacles that hampered native students' success. It may be assumed with some certainty that the same problems are encountered by university students. Among the survey's recommendations were the following ones: more involvement of the bands with the education endeavours of their people (in the form of bursaries and scholarships for successful students); provision of a native outreach worker to assist in areas such as finding accommodation, arranging transportation, procuring funding; general orientation sessions including financial management, human relations and college environment, Alcoholics Anonymous; measures (i.e. workshops, Native Club activities) to improve communication between natives and non-natives; and finally, more instruction in study skills.

A method that eliminates many of the above-mentioned problems while offering a university level education to natives even at remote locations consists in native outreach programs, now offered by all four of Alberta's universities. Off-campus courses were first begun by the University of Calgary in Morley (1973) where the Stoneys were offered a three-year program in education. Three Morley students and two other native students attending at the reserve have since completed Bachelor of Education degrees. Subsequent classes at Morley have been small, and the tribal administration is conducting an upgrading program in the hope of increasing the number of potential students for a future three-year program. No such program has yet been offered in Brocket. Other locations, where the University of Calgary is active, are Gleichen, Hobbema, Grouard, Fort McMurray and Fort Chipewyan. According to Evelyn Moore-Eyman, academic coordinator of Native Student Services (NSS) at the University of Calgary, outreach programs have already encouraged fifteen natives to continue their education. In 1982 nine social work students received a degree after completing their program on location. Fifty-seven students - a record number since 1973 - were enrolled on campus in fall 1981, the majority in education and social work; three were registered in law, and eight were studying in graduate degree programs. The retention rate among native students has much improved at the University of Calgary: From merely 20 per cent five years ago it has risen to over 80 per cent.

Another fairly recent phenomenon in the educational landscape is the establishment of Native American Studies Departments at regular universities. In 1974 only one university, Trent in Peterborough/Ontario, had such a program and actively recruited native people either as teachers or students. Later in the 1970s this trend picked up momentum in the west. The Native American Studies Department at the University of Lethbridge was founded in 1975. It offers courses in languages, history, art, literature, education, politics, sociology, law, and of course, Indian culture, all of which are taught from an Indian point of view. This program is not primarily job training oriented but rather adheres to a Liberal Arts philosophy. An advisory board made up of representatives from neighbouring Indian communities guides the program by pointing out educational needs of the people. These needs are then translated by the department into actual courses. Almost the entire faculty staff is native. One half of the students majoring in Native American Studies in Lethbridge are non-Indian, and many of the courses can be integrated into other programs. Most of the native students are from southern Alberta, but they also come from as far as Saskatchewan, Ontario, British Columbia and the Northwest Territories. Brandon, Manitoba, also has a Native Studies Program, and another one is in the process of being founded in the College of Arts and Science at the University of Saskatchewan in Saskatoon.

Discussions between the Federation of Saskatchewan Indians and the University of Regina led to the establishment of the Saskatchewan Indian Federated College in 1978. It offers programs leading to a B.A. in Indian Studies, a B.Ed. in Indian Education, an Indian Social Work Education Program, an Indian Management and Administration Program and an Indian Art Program. The Federated College has the only Indian Studies Bachelor Degree Program in North America which is entirely under the jurisdiction of the Indian people it serves. The College, although independent of the university, is academically integrated. A large part of its teaching activities takes place off-campus in the form of extension courses offered in Indian communities. Presently the Indian Chiefs of Alberta support a proposed Native College at the University of Alberta in Edmonton, similar to the Federated College in the neighbouring province.

The educational situation on both reserves and the educational opportunities available to young Stoneys and Peigan have been presented in some detail because there are so many ways in which education can either help or hamper the development of a community. Education does not just produce a certain kind of labour force, but it can condition a feeling of dejection or a feeling of self-esteem, depending on whether an educational system is imposed on one group by another or grows out of people's experiences and aspirations. Where the labour force is concerned there, too, is a great potential for both, frustration and fulfillment. If there is no existing economic structure to accommodate an improved labour force, or if concurrent factors needed to create such a structure - such as capital, markets, community support - fail to materialize, improved education is of no avail.

5.2.2.3 Labour Force: occupational Structure and economic and cultural Outlook

The Peigan and the Stoneys are no exception to the generalization that native people are over-represented in the so-called "unskilled" and "semi-skilled" area (e.g. service occupations, construction, forestry and logging, a variety of labour jobs) and underrepresented in the managerial, professional, clerical and sales areas. Even the present educational enrollment seems to indicate that a majority of band members is still being prepared to accept jobs at the semi-skilled level or lower.

Of the household heads interviewed on the Peigan Reserve 10 per cent were retired, and another 10 per cent were disabled. During their working life none of them had undergone any occupational training. The remaining household heads, 89 per cent of them male, could be classed as members of the Peigan workforce (1). Al-

---

1) Labour force/workforce is here defined as the Indian adult population in working age (16-64) rather than counting only those who are either employed or actively seeking work. This way the term also includes those who have become discouraged or succumbed to the welfare syndrome.

most 72 per cent were unskilled or semi-skilled; those who were employed worked as farm- or ranch-hands, busdrivers, road maintenance men or in other labour jobs. Another 11 per cent could be considered as skilled blue-collar workers, such as carpenters or plumbers. 13 per cent were engaged in "white-collar" occupations at the tribal administration; one half of this group had attended some college courses (such as management, accounting), the remainder had learnt "on-the-job". Finally, just over 4 per cent were undergoing some training: One individual was taking general upgrading courses; the other person was a college student.

Band statistics provide us with some information about the skill-levels achieved by two age groups within the Peigan labour force: those between the ages of 19 and 25 and between 26 and 45, accounting for 84.5 per cent of the total work force. In the younger group (19-25) only 19.1 per cent are classed as skilled whereas 69.9 per cent are unskilled and 11 per cent are still in school. The second age group (26-45) is composed of 35.5 per cent skilled workers, 55.7 per cent unskilled workers and 8.8 per cent in "white-collar" occupations. Even if we assume that those 11 per cent of the younger age group (19-25) still in school will proceed into skilled, white-collar or professional occupations the percentage in the unskilled category of almost 70 per cent is disconcertingly high.

The present unemployment rate on the Peigan Reserve is 70 per cent. With a work force of 713 individuals the reserve only offers 134 permanent positions; these would just barely satisfy 19 per cent of the labour force, provided that all these positions are staffed with band members. Presently many individuals hold jobs that lack any degree of permanence: Some are part of "make work" programs such as fencing, road maintenance and sanitation crews; others are seasonal in nature as for example ranching, farming and logging activities; and still others are temporary such as construction jobs involved with the upgrading of the L.N.I.D. works and the numerous positions created by the Weasel Valley Water Use Study. Off-reserve employment opportunities are not realized to any large degree; under 10 per cent of the Peigan work force are employed in neighbouring white communities.

The Stoney Reserves exhibit some similar characteristics, but the situation also differs in some ways. The Stoney labour force comprises some 900 individuals, of whom just over 300 are permanently employed, all on the reserves. Approximately half of these employees are female. An additional 100 are involved in temporary activities, mostly labour jobs sponsored by the Stoney Employment Program. Thus the reserve community accommodates about a third of its labour force in permanent employment. The unemployment rate is subject to seasonal fluctuations and varies between 50 and 60 per cent (taking into account self-employed individuals like ranchers). Information about the structure of the workforce is only available with regard to the employed section (permanent and temporary). 60 per cent are employed in unskilled or semi-skilled positions: in a variety of labour jobs, as pipe layers, janitors, security guards, truck drivers, ranch and forestry workers etc. 6 per cent are skilled blue-collar workers such as mechanics, welders, carpenters. 26 per cent work in such fields as childcare and community health and in conventional white-collar positions such as secretaries, office clerks, coordinators, receptionists and accountants. Another 6 per cent are employed in positions that are less easily categorized but which also qualify as white collar-jobs: linguists, researchers, fieldworkers, consultants and supervisory positions, where cultural knowledge and familiarity with the community are the vital ingredients. Less than 1 per cent qualify as professionals. Consideration of the unemployed section of the labour force would probably increase the percentage of the unskilled category. The survey results with the Chiniki Band reflected the above picture.

Thus the skill development and employment situation on the Peigan and Stoney Reserves is characterized by a vicious circle. On the one hand the scarcity of employment opportunities, especially for more highly skilled individuals, does little to boost people's motivation to improve their skills. On the other hand, a reservoir of skilled manpower is one of the vital factors needed to establish the groundwork for a viable economy. Despite the gradually improving educational opportunities for native people, training still is hard to come by for those who missed their chance once. Adult training courses would seem to be the answer, but most standard training programs, in the words of a Canada Manpower circular, "have excluded ... people having no steady occupational history or no definite early prospect of new employment ..." (Stangier, G., 1971, <u>Administration of Training Allowances</u>).

But there are other less tangible factors involved. The Stoneys and the Peigan are poorly equipped by their culture to copy western industrial development. Life in white society is highly compartmentalized. The economy is disassociated from all other activities and in itself corporatized, bureaucratized, professionalized and governed by its own laws which are in some cases diametrically opposed to norms and behaviour patterns a native person is accustomed to. In Indian cultures the economic, political, religious and social sphere constitute one integrated whole. Agressive and competitive behaviour in performing a task in which he has no intrinsic interest, would seem utterly incomprehensible to the native worker. Wealth as a symbol of success and prestige is not important to most Indians. Clock time holds little meaning for them, and certainly has no dollar value; as Zentner (1967: 84) puts it, "Time for them is not something to be treasured and conserved but rather something to be consumed." As Hawthorn (1966, Vol. 1: 58) and various other writers point out, Indians tend to be more uncomfortable working under the authority and supervision of a foreman than are whites. The latter have been trained and indoctrinated to accept authority in education, government and business, to make compromises and suffer indignities if necessary as a price for getting ahead. In Indian cultures the structures of status and authority do not coincide with the division of labour in a complex economy of large-scale operations; hence the exercise of authority in a working situation may be unacceptable because it is regarded as illegitimate (see also Pelletier 1971: 79-85). Social and family obligations may conflict with the rigidity of a working situation. Participation in certain kinds of activities, such as Indian days, sundances and rodeos is highly valued by many Stoneys and Peigan with the result that a person may quit his job so that he can attend such events. But there is evidence that economic development - be it extractive or secondary industries - can take place while accommodating such cultural traits like work as a communal rather than individual competitive experience or the adherence to informal time. Probably the best known example for such successful "alternative development" can be found on a reservation in South Dacota (Steiner 1968: 124):

> In the reeds along the banks of the Missouri River, up the bend from Running Water, in the town of Greenwood, is a unique factory.
> The factory on the old Yanktion Sioux Reservation is a fantasy of the Yanktion Sioux. It is a tribal dream that has been industrialized, like a prophet's vision of what the twentieth century could be. And yet it is as real as the electronic components it manufactures so idyllically - without a time clock.
> Every Sioux in the factory has his own desk. He comes to work when he wishes. He goes home when he wishes. He will work for twenty-four hours, round the clock, if he wishes; and then he won't work for a week. He will go fishing in the river, or take a correspondence course in missile engineering, or make love, or dance in the sun. He is paid at the end of the month for the work he has done, if he has done his work. No one asks him how, or when. He does not have to punch a time clock. There is none.
> There is not only no time clock in the factory, there are no time study engineers. There are no mangement-labor problems; for management and labor are both the same tribal entity. There are no traffic jams.

There are more examples like this, both in Canada and the United States. Pelletier (1971: 21 f) recounts an experience with Ontario Indians working at a sawmill in Longlac, who ended up much more productive when left to their own device without a foreman and without prescribed shifts. Not all these economic weddings of the tribal and the technological, the communal and the competitive, have been happy unions, and, unfortunately, there is no recent information on these enterprises, but they do show that there are alternative ways of doing things, which may satisfy all involved.

A final factor which must be mentioned is the impact of the historical interactions and relationships of the Stoneys and Peigan with whites. This factor is important because it influences the initiative which is so vital for any self-help. Over more than a century the contact situation has been characterized by weakness in the bargaining power of the Indian, and growing dependence on whites. To a degree this dependency pattern established itself during the fur trade era, but it was virtually perpetuated after the treaties with the onset of the reserve period. The Department of Indian Affairs still exerts a degree of authority over Indians, particularly over their economic matters, which has no counterpart in any other government agency with regard to non-Indians. A pervading paternalistic orientation and preemption of decisionmaking has characterized government policy towards Indian people. The continuing effect of such policy has not only been economic deprivation but also in many cases psychological crippling, evidenced in attitudes of dependency, apathy and irresponsibility. This phenomenon is one of the major roadblocks for those native individuals who work for the advancement of their people, and can only be understood in the light of history.

In conclusion it seems that the people themselves represent the most important asset of the Stoney and Peigan Reserves. But they also represent the most underutilized resource. This situation will only change if special programs are designed to fit the needs of disadvantaged groups such as untrained Indian adults, and if native people are given the opportunity and the means to do things in their own way, be it in the areas of education or economic development.

5.2.3 The Capital

5.2.3.1 The economic Situation of Stoney and Peigan Households

The nature of the economic situation of Stoney and Peigan households is partly reflected by their occupational and employment situation. With an overrepresentation in unskilled and semi-skilled job categories and an unemployment rate between 60 and 70 per cent it is fairly evident that the average Stoney and Peigan income is considerably lower than the average Canadian income (1). The major portion of the Indian labour force on both reserves is without gainful employment and at the same time unable to sustain itself by ranching or farming. Consequently they have to rely on some other source of income, usually social assistance.

The Stoneys, however, are in a different position. Their natural gas royalties provide them with a substantial tribal income which is shared among the community by means of bi-weekly per capita payments, investment in economic projects, and works of a capital nature. When the Stoneys started their full-time interest payments two years ago, thus enabling each single member of the tribe to benefit from the communally owned resource, they became independent from social assistance payments, and for the first time even unemployed reserve residents came to receive an annual income substantially above the poverty line.

Members of the Peigan Tribe are less fortunate. Here a large proportion of the population does depend on the Department of Indian and Northern Affairs Social Assistance Program. The rates and regulations for this program are set by the department which uses provincial regulations as guidelines. The program is administered by the Peigan Band Administration which, of course, is accountable to Indian Affairs. Social Assistance covers basic needs such as food, clothing, shelter, fuel, utilities, and personal and household supplies. Its function is to make available to individuals and families assistance necessary "to maintain health, safety and family unity". Band members relying on this source of income receive an annual income considerably below the Statistics Canada Poverty Line.

---

1) Due to the confidential nature of the matter, no income figures will be revealed.

5.2.3.2   Band Funds

As for all of Canada's Treaty Indians, the Stoneys' und Peigan's band funds are held in Ottawa. Under federal direction their accumulated finance goes into what is commonly called the "trust fund". There are two funds for each tribe, namely the capital account and the revenue account. The capital account is made up of funds derived from the sale of surrendered lands, oil and gas royalties and bonuses. Basically it is composed of the conversion of any depreciating assets to cash. The revenue account is obtained from all forms of leases, permits and contracts entered into, including sales of natural resources. For example the revenue created by oil exploration leases on the Peigan Reserve went straight to Ottawa to be administered at the discretion of the federal government. Money accumulating in the trust fund only draws twelve per cent interest compared to nineteen per cent in regular financial institutions. The revenue account sustains the operations of the reserves and is supplemented by an annual transfer from the capital account and by government appropriations and grants. The capital account is used to finance works of a capital nature on the reserves, such as houses, roads, water and sewage facilities.

The extent of fiscal control over Indian bands exercised by the federal Department of Indian Affairs is unparalleled. Despite the chronical shortage of funds with most bands the paramount problem is not so much "having" money as access to and control of the financial resource, including the choice of projects to be supported. Governmental control over the bands' financial management is not confined to grants and appropriations out of the Indian Affairs budget – which often take the form of separate agreements with rigid guidelines and strict accountability –, but it includes the money accrued from Indian assets. Yet the extent of restraint exercised by the department varies according to the degree of financial independence achieved by the reserves.

Thanks to their gas royalties the Stoneys are in the fortunate position of being virtually independent from Indian Affairs appropriations. They only receive "token funding" for administrative purposes, while social assistance was cut off in 1979, after the Stoneys implemented full-time interest payments to all band members out of the natural gas royalties. The tribe controls its own revenue account, whereas the capital account is still administered by the Department of Indian Affairs. The Indian Act (Section 64) stipulates that a maximum of 50 per cent of a band's capital may be distributed on a per capita basis. At the beginning of each fiscal year the band council draws up a budget, which must be approved by Ottawa prior to implementation. While the Stoneys enjoy comparative freedom in deciding how their own money is invested, their situation is still characterized by strict accountability to Ottawa. In fact, after a Supreme Court ruling in British Columbia in mid-1981, charging the Department of Indian Affairs with mismanagement of trust funds, the top departmental officials in Ottawa have decided to be much more cautious in approving release of funds to bands and much more thorough and demanding of bands in their accounting procedures. Bands on high revenue producing reserves are especially hard hit by these measures, as the new procedures are causing serious administrative and cash flow problems (<u>Kainai News</u>, June No 1, 1982).

The problems faced by the Peigan are somewhat different and more typical for those reserves – who are in the majority - lacking high revenue producing natural resources. Prior to the beginning of each fiscal year they are issued a financial lay-out by Indian Affairs stating exactly how many funds have been earmarked for various purposes: social assistance, housing, recreation, education, policing, economic development etc. Within these confines the council decides on a budget, which must be approved by Ottawa. In other words, most of the funds are nondiscretionary, their allocation being determined by statute. These vital decisions are made thousands of miles away from where the real problems occur and have to be filtered through the district, regional and head offices of the Department of Indian Affairs. It goes without saying that this procedure places major constraints on planning expenditures to meet special local needs or circumstances (for example housing shortage). Even more disconcerting is the availability of funds for social assistance rather than for economic development. It must suffice here to say that for the fiscal year 1982/83 the respective ratio for the Peigan equalled 16 : 1, the money available for economic development being a mere token sum.

It is difficult not to suspect a purpose behind all this. The matter of constraint over Indian bands' financial management appears to be simply another social control mechanism. In earlier times the social control functions of Indian administration included restriction of movement, forced indoctrination with Euro-Canadian ideology and involuntary enfranchisement. Today such tactics lack legitimacy and have largely been replaced with what may be termed socio-fiscal control. A very important aspect of socio-fiscal control on the reserve level is the dependency created by lengthy periods of resort to welfare payments. As confirmed by Ponting and Gibbins (1980: 125), prolonged welfare is quite capable of draining individuals of the initiative and sense of self-esteem that are necessary for launching any challenge to the political or administrative status quo. Another aspect is the paradox inherent in the fact that the reserves' leadership is accountable to a remote government in Ottawa rather than to their own electorate. This situation bears features of a "divide and conquer" strategy, as there is much suspicion found in the communities about "where all the money goes". While corruption and political favouritism are encountered on reserves the same as in the larger political arena, there is a strong tendency on the grassroot level to place all blame squarely on the shoulders of Chief(s) and Council for a situation which is clearly out of their hands. Among the Stoneys and Peigan there is a general awareness that their special status as Treaty Indians is threatened, but other than that their political clairvoyance is understandably limited. And even for a more sophisticated mind it is somewhat hard to understand why under a declared program of local self-government of Indian reserves the Indian Affairs department still determines the policy which then is simply administered by the band staff. This becomes most blatantly open in the area of financial management.

5.2.3.3   Potential outside Sources of Funding

Access to and control over financial resources are indispensible for making the reserves economically viable. As indicated above, the budget available for economic development of the communities is limited, especially for reserves with a smaller capital and revenue account like the Peigan Reserve. In practice this means a restraint on number and scale of band enterprises, an incapability of existing enterprises to pay their workers competitive wages and limited power of the band government to effectively assist band members who want to get started in their own business.

Indian Act stipulations make it very difficult for native people to approach traditional financing mechanisms because they are unable to provide the needed collateral. Indian land or Indian property on a reserve is not subject to pledge or mortgage, and therefore, cannot be put up as security. To meet this limitation and others, such as lack of business experience and poor physical accessibility of some reserves, the Department of Indian Affairs introduced the Indian Economic Development Fund in 1970. In one form or another an Indian loan fund had been used for economic development since the 1950s (then the Revolving Fund, now the Indian Economic Development Fund). The Indian Economic Development Fund is project-rather than program-oriented and was conceived in the absence of any comprehensive socio-economic development program. It consists of three components: the Direct Loan Fund, the Guaranteed Loan Fund, and Grants and Contributions. Loans under the Direct Loan Fund are obtained through the Department of Indian Affairs. Loans acquired under the Guaranteed Loan Fund are negotiated through commercial banks or lending agencies, with security provided by a government guarantee. Both direct and guaranteed loans are obtained at more or less commercial rates and terms. Grants and contributions complement the loans by providing non-repayable funds for development purposes. With regard to the Indian Economic Development Fund it has to be borne in mind though that it is an integral part of the same federal government department whose background and ideology were spelled out in the previous chapter. The budgetary structure of the reserves in question and its rigidity is only a reflection of the overall situation in the department responsible for it. Almost three-quarters of the Indian and Inuit Affairs Program (within the Department of Indian and Northern Affairs) expenditures are considered non-discretionary, being devoted to such programs as education, social assistance and services, housing and community infrastructure. Of the remaining discretionary funds almost a third goes into administration costs (for example "core funding" to pay chief and council and administrative staff, which is supplemented by the reserves' revenue accounts), while most of the rest is usually devoted to economic development (DIAND 1980: 112). During the 1970s economic development doubled its share of the Indian and Inuit Affairs Program budget, but at less than 10 per cent at the end of the decade, it was surpassed by the administration costs which the program incurred through its headquarters, regional and district offices. Frideres (1974: 170) comments on the Indian Economic Development Fund that generally the maximum loan is $ 10,000 - although the maximum amount is not stipulated in the Indian Economic Development Direct Loan Order - to be repaid with interest within five years. There does not seem to have been much progress in the subsequent years: During 1979-80 this fund was used to provide 193 direct loans totalling $ 2.62 million, an average loan would amount to $ 13,575. Very few economically viable ventures can be established with this kind of capital which must be repaid, with interest, within a short period of time. In today's agricultural system it takes hundreds of thousands of dollars for machinery, buildings, labour and working capital to get started in either farming or ranching. Non-agricultural projects tend to be equally expensive. Guaranteed loans from conventional lenders tend to be somewhat larger than direct loans from Indian Affairs. Due to serious financial mismanagement in the 1970s the Indian Economic Development Fund has been a source of major problems within the program. Following a review in 1976, investment dropped off by about 40 per cent, as emphasis was placed on smaller projects and non-repayable contributions. Until the state of confusion is rectified it is unlikely that the Treasury Board will approve major new initiatives in economic development loans in the 1980s (Ponting and Gibbins 1980: 122).

Thus it becomes abundantly clear, that it is simply not possible for a single government department to handle Indian economic development needs on a national basis. At the same time, Indians can only counter government socio-fiscal control by developing even a small measure of fiscal autonomy through the diversification of funding sources. This might be achieved through the involvement of other government departments, provincial and federal, through the assistance of non-Indian support organizations such as philanthropic foundations or through developing sharing mechanisms whereby the few wealthy bands assist poor bands. The latter two possibilities, though, do not seem too realistic. The situation also calls for a coordinated delivery system, combining resources, funding, and training.

During the last couple of years the Indian Affairs Program has no longer been the exclusive federal agent for the delivery of programs to Indians. Twenty-one per cent of expenditures to Indians were made through other agencies in 1978-79. Programs from other departments have been initiated during the last decade which have a more general focus than Indian economic development, for example short-term job creation by Canada Works, Young Canada Works, Local Employment Assistance Program (LEAP), Summer Youth Employment, and Federal Labour Intensive Program; labour market skill development through training programs such as Canada Manpower Training Program (CMTP), Canada Manpower Industrial Training Program (CMITP) and Outreach, adminstered by the Canada Employment and Immigration Commission.

Some of the more interesting and comprehensive programs to boost Indian economic development have been those administered by the Department of Regional Economic Expansion (DREE), particularly Special ARDA (ARDA stands for Agricultural and Rural Development Act). Operating under cost-sharing agreements with the provincial governments, this program seeks to improve the income and employment opportunities of people in rural areas by providing financial and other assistance to create job opportunities. In British Columbia Indian input in the decision-making process is made possible by cooperation with the provincial native organizations. Unfortunately no Special ARDA-agreement has yet been signed by the Province of Alberta, although there is considerable native pressure on the provincial government to do so. But Indian people in this province have been in touch with other programs administered by DREE, such as the Prairie Farm Rehabilitation Administration (PFRA), who agreed to undertake the engineering feasibility study for the Peigan within the framework of their Weasel Valley Water Use Study.

A final federal source of assistance for Indians that should be mentioned here, is the Federal Business Development Bank. The objectives of this institution are to promote and assist in the establishment and development of business enterprises (primary, secondary and service industries) by providing them with financial and management services. It supplements such services available from others and gives particular attention to the needs of smaller enterprises. The Federal Business Development Bank also offers a counselling service to assist small businesses in improving their management.

Where provincial services or assistance to native people are concerned, there is a mutual reluctance to provide or accept this assistance. The provincial position is that Section 91 (24) of the British North America Act gives the federal government responsibility for Indians on and off reserves, and therefore, the federal government is responsible for either directly providing services or covering 100 per cent of costs of services provided by the province. This position also affects economic development assistance. Likewise, Indians will not accept any federal or provincial position that will diminish what they understand to be the federal government's comprehensive responsibility for them nor any program that tends to reinforce integration or assimilation of Indians into the non-Indian population.

Finally, two programs in Alberta that are purely Indian-oriented are the Alberta Indian Agricultural Development Corporation (AIADC) and the Business Assistance For Native Albertans Corporation. The Alberta Indian Agricultural Development Corporation was designed after the Manitoba and Saskatchewan Indian Agriculture Programs Inc., which are Indian-owned corporations providing development, extension and funding services to Indian farmer clients. As a joint effort of the Treaty Seven Agricultural Committee and the Department of Indian Affairs the AIADC incorporated as a non-profit corporation in 1979. Its main objective is the provision of financial assistance in the form of grants, contributions and loans and of management and counselling resources to Indian farmers and ranchers and Indian band councils to develop the agricultural resources on Indian reserves. The corporation's activities only went underway in 1981, and it is too soon to draw any conclusions about its effectiveness. One of its major drawbacks is its dependence on federal funding, largely out of the Indian Economic Development Fund. Only $ 750,000 was allocated to the program during the fiscal year of 1981/82. Financial assistance was meant to constitute one of the program's major components. Grants are used as equity capital to allow Indian clients to obtain loans from traditional lending institutions. In some cases, the farmers are required to take training in basic farming techniques in return for the maximum $ 20,000 grants.

The Business Assistance For Native Albertans Corporation (BANAC), incorporated in June 1980, received § 1.2 million in funds from the provincial government in an effort to create better business opportunities for small native businessmen. BANAC was not set up as a source of funding, but rather offers consulting services on how to increase the profit (of any kind of business) and of how to have access to money through the private sector. BANAC plans to expand with field offices throughout the province, in the 1982/83 fiscal year. The fact that BANAC is neither native-initiated nor controlled by Indians or Metis, but is a provincially run organization, still seems to be a problem (Nations' Ensign, March 1982: 5). It is not being supported by the Indian Association of Alberta. Also there is some confusion among native people about the type of business assistance available through BANAC, and about the fact that it is not a source of funds. Moreover, BANAC duplicates to some degree the services of the Indian Equity Foundation, which offers business expertise and funding.

One problem that all these sources of funding and other assistance to Indians seem to have in common, is their perceived accessibility and native people's scant knowledge even of their existence. Among the Stoney and Peigan residents it was found that only very few individuals have ever sought the services of such institutions as the Federal Business Development Bank and the Alberta Indian Agricultural

Development Corporation. A large majority either had not even heard of them or was very doubtful about how to approach them.

5.3   The Renewable Resource Sector: Potential and Economic Activities

5.3.1   Livestock Production

The Peigan and the Stoney Reserves are situated in one of Alberta's main rangeland areas. "Rangelands are those areas of the world, which by reason of physical limitations - low and erratic precipitation, rough topography, poor drainage, or cold temperatures - are unsuited to cultivation and which are a source of forage for free-ranging native and domestic animals, as well as a source of wood products, water and wildlife" (Stoddart, Smith and Box 1975: 3). This characterization in terms of physical limitations fully applies to the Stoney Reserves, and, to a lesser degree, to the Peigan Reserves, the larger one of which does contain arable land.

The general trend for the Morley Reserve proper is for the productive woodlands to be concentrated on the highlands to the north and south of the Bow River (14,367 hectar or 35 per cent of the total area), and for these to grade into unproductive woodlands (12,222 hectar), thence to range or rough grazing lands (12,262 hectar or 30 per cent), as the elevation decreases and the river is approached. Scatterings of unproductive woodlands occur in both productive woodland areas and rangeland. Due to the severe seasonal fluctuations in the water level of the Bow River, much of the area immediately adjacent to the river consists of unvegetated exposures of river gravels and silts.

As outlined in a previous chapter the grasslands of the Stoney Reserves are generally dominated by rough fescue. In a well managed condition this grassland is the most productive of all native rangeland in Alberta, but a large proportion of the Stoney lands is in a state of severe overgrazing. The land productivity for grazing is usually expressed as carrying capacity. Carrying capacity or grazing capacity has come to be regarded as "the maximum animal numbers which can graze each year on a given area of range, for a specific number of days, without inducing a downward trend in forage production, forage quality, or soil" (ibid.: 183). This device takes into consideration the vegetation - usually the climax community -, the soil situation and the climatic conditions, as they affect the vegetation cover, since overutilization of the forage is to be prevented in all but the most extreme drought. As will be outlined later, carrying capacity must not be confused with recommendable stocking rates. The Alberta Department of Lands and Forests (Range, its Nature and Use, 1970, map on: 21) depicting grazing capacity zones in Alberta, places the Stoney Reserves into zones four and five. Zone four (rough fescue prairie, foothills) has an average stocking rate of 0.7 hectar (1.7 acres) per A.U. (1) per month (= 16 hectar/39.6 acres per A.U. in a 12 months grazing system). Elgaard (1968: 2) ascribes an average carrying capacity of 9.7 hectar (24 acres) per A.U. per year to the foothills ranching region. In their study on Range Management of Grasslands and Adjacent Parklands in the Prairie Provinces, Campbell et al. (1962, map on: 26) place our study area into a carrying capacity zone of < 0.9 hectar (< 2.25 acres) per A.U.M. (< 10.9 hectar/27 acres per A.U. per year), but the same study also points out the capability differences between range sites within the fescue prairie: site 1 with 0.45 hectar (1.1 acres) per A.U.M. (5.3 hectar or 13.2 acres per A.U. per year) and site 2 with 0.73 hectar (1.8 acres) per A.U.M. (8.7 hectar or 21.6 acres per A.U. per year); and these values are not even extremes. Hence it is obvious that overall values are of little use as a planning tool.

There are two studies dealing with the grazing potential of the Stoney Reserves in somewhat more detail: the Underwood McLellan and Associates Limited Land Use Study (1969) and R. England's thesis (1966), covering only the Morley Reserve proper. With regard to the soil situation at least both take into account range sites.

---

1) A.U. = Animal Unit, considered to be one mature cow with calf or their equivalent (for example one horse); A.U.M. = Animal Unit per month.

Both include into their grazing appraisal not only grassland and parkland, but also forest lands, which - even when producing commercial timber - can be utilized by livestock on a multiple use basis. England arrives at his results by the correllation of various sources. To assess the grazing capacity of open rangeland, he utilizes the present cover type (mapped by him), a map of soil capability ratings compiled in the 1943 soil survey of the Rosebud and Banff sheets and some results of the Campbell study. The rates he uses for estimating the carrying capacity of invaded rangeland and commercial forest are based again on the soil rating map and on data from grazing allotments in the adjacent Provincial Forest: the Ghost grazing allotment to the north of the reserve and the Jumpingpound grazing allotment to the south. England's computer maps and associated data do not lend themselves to ready analysis of regional differences in grazing capacity, but rather to local appraisals; they shall not be elaborated here. Underwood McLellan and Associates Limited employ the soil classification of the Canada Land Inventory and base their cattle carrying capacities on these soil classes. The values are given as acres per head per annum. With regard to the anticipated twelve months grazing period, however, it should be borne in mind, that a twelve months grazing system is not feasible in areas other than open range (England, p. 21). Under brush and forest cover, greater snow accumulation and persistence of snow cover inhibits year-round utilization of the understory. Here carrying capacity should be calculated for a seven months grazing system, and allowance be made for winter feed.

The main Morley Reserve displays rather favourable conditions in its eastern extremity and in the lowland of the Bow River valley with 10-12 hectar (25-30 acres) per head per annum, the carrying capacity being considerably higher (namely 2-4 hectar/5-10 acres per head per annum) where there occur patches of improved pasture or extraordinarily favourable soil conditions, coupled with level terrain, like in the extreme east of the reserve, and much lower (namely 20-24 hectar/50-60 acres per head per annum) where there are islands of brush and poplar. Large parts of the northwest and southwest are rated as not suitable for permanent grazing at all (coinciding on the map with areas of productive woodland); these areas are interspersed with land of low carrying capacity, for example 24-28 hectar (60-70 acres) per head per annum in the northwest, and 16-20 hectar (40-50 acres) northeast of Broken Leg Lake and in the vicinity of the Chiniki Lake Road in the southwest (coinciding with unproductive woodland).

The Rabbit Lake Reserve, which is approximately 85 per cent productive woodland, has a very limited grazing potential with a carrying capacity of 20-28 hectar (50-70 acres) per head per annum in some parts of its two main valleys, and some tiny pockets of more favourable conditions with 8-12 hectar (20-30 acres) per head per annum. Its main potential lies in commercial timber production and recreational development, not in livestock economy. The same applies to the Bighorn Reserve, where grazing is more or less restricted to the North Saskatchewan River Valley. The area can maintain twenty-six animals. Most of the flatland of the Eden Valley Reserve is rangeland with a grazing capacity of 8-16 (20-40 acres) per head per annum. The natural grasslands of the Hughes Ranch maintain cattle at the rate of 10 hectar (25 acres) per head per annum, its improved pasture at the rate of only 4 hectar (10 acres) per animal unit per year.

This evaluation can only serve as a very rough indication of the grazing potential of the Stoney Reserves. The actual development of their range resource will have to rely on a more detailed analysis of range sites in each case and above all, on a careful consideration of the range condition. The greater the difference between the present and potential forage production of a site, the greater the discrepancy will be between carrying capacity and recommended stocking rates (see Alberta Guide to recommended Stocking Rates in Smoliak et al. 1976: 23). Other factors likely to affect recommendable stocking rates - besides the anticipated grazing system - are water development, salting, fencing, herding and riding, trail system etc., these being measures which influence the distribution of grazing animals to prevent local overgrazing. Whatever grazing systems will be employed to manage the forage resource - probably deferred-rotation and rest-rotation rather than continuous grazing -, in each case the system will have to be tailored to an individual enterprise or grazing allotment to be effective.

The previous discussion was centred around maintenance of the present cover conditions. Yet in many cases a manipulation of the range vegetation is feasible to increase the output. Among the various means of range improvement and plant cover manipulation two in particular stand out in their applicability to the Stoney Reserves: brush control and the replacement of native grasses with tame pasture. The Underwood McLellan and Associates study stresses that there are areas in the eastern sector of the main Morley Reserve, but also in the west, along the Transcanada Highway, which would respond favourably to re-seeding in productive rangeland. Selected brush clearance and improvement is suggested for various sections in the southwestern part of the reserve like land northeast of Chiniki Lake, for land north and east of the Morley settlement and a large block of land surrounding Potts Lake. These areas are interspersed with bluffs of unproductive timber.

The practice of replacing native range with tame pasture - reseeding with cultivated grasses rather than native species - was regarded mainly as a means of rejuvenating submarginal cultivated lands and depleted rangeland. As late as 1962 Johnston and Wilson (p. 11) wrote:

> An improper concept of reseeding has developed. We tend to think in terms of reseeding the poorest sites that are not now producing native grasses and probably will never produce anything worth while, whereas it is only better rangeland that has much potential. This still does not mean that we should plough up good grass, but it does mean that where the cover has been devastated by overgrazing, and a population of persistent but unproductive species is all that remains, cultivated grasses can be used.

Experiments in Saskatchewan had then shown considerable yield increases from reseeding, but these gains were short-lived, and, as the authors (ibid.) emphasize "it is important to recognize that any increased carrying capacity realized in the early years of a new stand can be maintained only with continual reseeding, or perhaps fertilization". Although the amount of capital and labour (seedbed preparation) involved still necessitates careful consideration of such an undertaking, a broader appreciation of the potential of tame pasture seems to have developed. In the Canadian prairies the main objectives of the employment of introduced grasses are an increase in forage yields and an extension of the grazing season. Crested wheatgrass (Agropyron cristatum L. Gaertn. and Agropyron desertorum Fisch. Schult.) and Russian wildrye (Elymus junceus Fisch.) are the most commonly used species for range reseeding. With regard to forage yields it was found, that crested wheatgrass produces about twice as much forage per hectar as native range, and it can be stocked three times as heavily (Lodge, Smoliak and Johnston 1972). Smoliak and Slen (1974) found that established pastures of Russian wildrye produced from five to seven times as much gain per acre as did native range when grazed by yearling steers during a six months grazing season. Both grasses have been particularly successful in complementary grazing systems with native range, by filling in seasonal deficiencies of the native species and thus extending the grazing season: Being a cool-season grass, crested wheatgrass grows rapidly early in spring. This rapid growth and its palatability make it ideal for early spring grazing. The peak forage production period for crested wheatgrass is in May, whereas native grassland does not reach its peak until June. Thus crested wheatgrass pastures make it possible to defer spring grazing for native range, then in its most vulnerable state. Russian wildrye is best grazed during late summer and fall, due to its comparatively high nutritious value during this season, when native grasses are low in protein and phosphorus, and high in carbohydrates. The experiments leading to the results outlined above have been mainly conducted on shortgrass and mixed prairie, but should be equally applicable to fescue grassland: The superiority in forage yield of the introduced grasses is probably reduced, rough fescue being more vigorous and higher yielding than the more xeric species. In a complementary grazing system though crested wheatgrass can fulfill the same function in fescue grassland as in the more arid parts of the northern prairie, since the production peak of rough fescue falls into July (Lodge et al. 1971, graph: 24). With regard to fall grazing in the fescue prairie and parkland these authors suggest creeping red fescue, brome grass, intermediate wheat grass, pubescent wheat grass, alsike clover, and rambler alfalfa as the best pasture crops to complement range (ibid.: 27).

The second suggestion to manipulate range vegetation on the Stoney Reserves was concerned with brush control. It has been estimated that 200 to 300 per cent increases in carrying capacity are possible by eradication of woody species (Johnston and Wilson 1962: 11). As outlined in Chapter 5.1.4 aspen vegetation has a natural tendency to invade and succeed the prairie vegetation, and its progress has been accelerated in historical times by the extermination of the buffalo (England and de Vos 1969: 89) and the virtual cessation of once common prairie fires, frequently started by careless individuals, both Indian and immigrant, and by wood and coal burning locomotives. According to Johnston and Smoliak (1968: 406) brush invasion is still actively underway; in the southwestern Alberta parkland the rate of conversion of grassy range to trees approximates 0.75 per cent of the total area per year. The presence of woody vegetation on rangeland depresses its productivity in various ways: Cattle do not browse extensively; heavy invasion can inhibit cattle access to natural grass understory, and the growth of palatable grasses under brush and poplar is limited by the competition of brush and poplar for moisture and light. There are two basic methods for eradicating and controlling brush: chemical and mechanical, the latter being the more costly. When removal of brush and poplar is carried out to convert an area of invaded rangeland to native grasses, chemical methods are employed as much as possible. According to England (1966: 35) the reason for this is that release of native range does not result in a large increase in return; consequently costs must be kept to a minimum. Large aspen, however, cannot be killed satisfactorily by aerial spraying, and the most feasible approach to such areas is to clear them by the most economical means possible, ball and chain, and then control regrowth by aerial spraying. Spraying is an adequate means of controlling regrowth if applied every four years. In the standard procedure in southwestern Alberta, as described by Johnston and Smoliak (1968: 404), aspen and willow are "walked down" by bulldozer during the winter, piled, and later burned. Usually the land is broken and cultivated for a year or two to control regrowth of aspen or to prepare a seedbed in cleared willow sites. A cereal crop may be seeded during these years and utilized for pasture, hay or grain. Afterwards the land is seeded to an adapted grass-legume mixture, for example Carlton bromegrass (Bromus inermis Leyss.) and rambler alfalfa (Medicago sativa L.). Russian wildrye and rambler alfalfa have been seeded on shallower soils, especially when fall and winter pasture was required. The herbicide usually employed to kill willow and aspen regrowth is 2.4-D ester, applied at 32 oz/acre. After clearing follow-up operations as described above are crucial to make the undertaking a success. Johnston and Smoliak (1968: 406) found that a generalized sequence of ecological succession in the foothills appears to be from grass to willows to aspen to conifers. Willow is susceptible to 2.4-D. Thus it is felt that local infestations of willow should be controlled with chemicals before stands grow to where mechanical clearing becomes a necessity.

On the basis of their land capability classification Underwood McLellan and Associates concluded that Morley, including Rabbit Lake, could support some 1,800 animal units, Eden Valley 148, and the Bighorn Reserve 26. These figures are based on the present vegetation cover without anticipating any betterment measures or plant cover manipulation; but it must be emphasized once more that they are not based on a proper range survey with an examination of range sites and an analysis of the range condition. Moreover they assume a twelve months grazing system which is not feasible in many parts of the reserves. England (1966) focussing only on Morley proper, arrives at a considerably higher figure: open rangeland under a twelve month grazing system / 1,742 A.U., under a seven months grazing system / 2,986 A.U.; invaded rangeland under a seven months grazing system / 378 A.U.; commercial forest land under a seven months grazing system / 798 A.U.; total 2,918 or 4,162 A.U. Under these conditions all land would be stocked with grazing animals and none be left for hay production. According to this author, through manipulation of the present cover type on all soil capability classes with exception of class 2 (not Canada Land Inventory but Wyatt et al. 1943), namely conversion to tame pasture, plus allocation of land to hay production for the entire cattle population in winter, the Morley Reserve could support 10,424 A.U. under a seven months grazing system and produce 10,424 tons of hay per annum to feed them in winter. Considering the present state of affairs this suggestion is of course hypothetical. Underwood McLellan and Associates assessed the potential capacity at

Morley, utilizing range management and husbandry techniques as 6,000 A.U.

But whatever management goal is envisaged, a range management policy would have to be developed. A community pasture which was run on a communal or co-operative basis during summer, was in existence during the late 1960s. Located in the northwestern sector of the main reserve, it was used by the individual cattle owners, who paid rent per head of cattle. Stockmen were paid from the rentals, and a pasture manager formulated and implemented a policy for the use of the pasture. Considering the small size of most individual herds, the principle of management policies and community herds could be extended to cover the livestock economy of the whole reserve and also Eden Valley and Bighorn (Underwood McLellan and Associates 1969: 117). This would entail the formulation of an agricultural and husbandry policy and a coordinated management of the agricultural resources of the reserves. The report gives no suggestions as to the kind of management policy to be realized, but it should be an effective tool to safeguard recommendable stocking rates and the implementation of suitable grazing systems and certain range mangement practices. It could also result in the formation of a cooperative livestock enterprise whereby cattle owners could pool their animals, and pay a rent to have them managed through a central management. If a cattle owner did not join the cooperative, he would still be obliged to look after his herds within the management policies set down for the reserve as a whole. Along with this voluntary cooperative the establishment of a band herd is recommended to be managed under the same principles. Further, the study suggests that any owner, whether a member of the cooperative or not, would be required to pay rent to the band for grazing lands and hay, the use of buildings and equipment, so that the operation becomes self-sustaining and finally makes a profit.

As to present agricultural activities on the Stoney Reserves there are no recent reliable data available with regard to the number of horses, cattle, cattle owners or size of herds. When the Underwood McLellan and Associates study was undertaken, there were approximately 600 head of cattle at Morley, of which 125 were owned by non-Indians. Presently there are no non-Indian owned cattle on the reserve, whereas the number of Stoney cattle is likely to have declined (Sykes Powderface, personal communication). In 1969 there were fifty to sixty cattle owners, with the largest owner having forty to fifty head of cattle. The overall small size of individual herds still applies. The enterprises are cow-calf operations. In the 1960s and early 1970s the individual herds were run together during the summer under the supervision of band paid stockmen, and in winter, each owner looked after his own cattle. In recent years, however, even the pooling of herds during the summer has been discontinued, so that each owner now operates his own herd throughout the year. Land that could be termed "community pasture" is more or less spotty in distribution, for example approximately 810 hectar (2,000 acres) north of the Morley settlement; many individuals use it during the summer months. Another 2,020 hectar (5,000 acres) of hay meadow west of Potts Lake are also communally utilized.

The individual holdings are scattered throughout the rangeland and unproductive woodland. In the Chiniki sample interviewed there were three individuals who could be classed as full-time ranchers; their herds counted between thirty-five and fifty head of cattle. But many other individuals with different sources of income also keep cattle in smaller numbers, between one and fifteen. This applies even more to the ownership of horses, with 75 per cent of the households owning horses (up to thirty) compared to 44 per cent grazing cattle. A veneration for horses is found in all socio-economic strata. While some individuals only own a saddle horse or cutting and rodeo horses, others pasture a great number of unbroken animals, the exact quantity of which they do not know. Little selective breeding is practised, though. The majority of the cattle population are of the Hereford type; in summer band bulls may be rented for a fee of $ 5, but there is no specific breeding policy. Marketing of the stock is not pooled, but takes place individually, mainly through public stockyards in Calgary. With very few exceptions, where the pasture is rotated, no grazing systems are implemented, and no measures are taken to manipulate the present vegetation cover in any way. The application of any range management practices would necessitate a sound system of fencing. On the Stoney Reserve, although in the process of being improved it still is in poor repair with the result that many animals, especially horses, roam all over the reserve, a great number getting killed on the roads and railway tracks. This state of affairs is also likely to complicate the stock's supply with winterfeed. Many Stoney livestock owners make their own hay; of those who do not, most buy their supply off the reserve. While a few of the Stoney ranchers would be interested in increasing the productivity of their livestock operation (both as a sideline or full-time activity) beyond a state of self-sufficiency, the basic orientation appears to be a desire to produce enough for one's own and one's family's needs. The shortage of land, the small size of herds and the fact that cattle are often being kept as a "sideline" would indicate that cooperative management might be a sensible idea. But there seems to be a split in the community with some being willing to or even interested in trying it out once more, while about the same number express a preference for looking after their stock themselves, some because they simply enjoy it, others because they do not trust cooperatives. There also is a pronounced wariness of the imposition of a range management policy.

Half of the overheads of the individual operations are carried by the band: capital cost and maintenance of all farm machinery and implements, the cost of buildings and fences, veterinarian fees and medicine, salt, winter supply of hay etc. The only direct contribution made by the cattle owner to band funds is a nominal fee per head paid when cattle are sold under permit. Thus the Stoney cattle owners do not have to account for the normal operational costs of ranching enterprises. This situation presents a false picture of the economics of livestock operations on the reserve: Ranches which would not be economical to manage off the reserve due to the small size of the herds and the resultant high overheads and low margins of profit, may still pay their way for the Stoney ranchers as one half of their overheads is carried for them.

But we must be aware of the fact that there is much more involved than simple economics. Looking at the situation only in terms of economic feasibility means looking at it from an ethnocentric perspective. To avoid this it is necessary to consider what role the Indian community plays for the individual. Although there are major cultural differences between tribes some statements by Steiner (1968: 140) seem generally applicable:

> Everything in tribal life is based on the community's protection of the individual. The tribe shelters a man's family with the umbrella of the kinship family. The tribe nourishes a man's well-being in time of failure with its built-in brotherhood and neighborliness ... Communality of tribalism does not diminish the Indian's individuality. On the contrary it protects him socially and thus frees him individually.

Communal ownership of resources is integral part of this maxim. As was shown with regard to land, its realization under modern circumstances is not without problems. But due to their wealth in natural gas the Stoneys are financially better off than the Peigan. Thus in a way the income accruing from a communally owned and quite substantial non-renewable resource is used to somehow offset resource shortages in other areas (such as land). As was shown in Chapter 5.2.1.2 there is no chance that the reserve could accommodate all those who want to engage in livestock raising on an economic unit basis. But in the protective environment of the reserve Euro-Canadian economic laws somehow cease to apply, and the individual - benefitting from a tribally owned resource - still has the freedom of engaging in an activity that would prove uneconomic under off-reserve competitive conditions.

The livestock operations at Eden Valley are financed the same way as at the Morley Reserve, but there is a more advanced degree of management. The individual herds, totalling about 420, are run on a cooperative type of basis throughout the year. The herds are looked after by band stockmen in the summer, while they graze on the Eden Valley Reserve proper; they are wintered at the Hughes Ranch, where there is not only natural forage, but also some 65 hectar (160 acres) producing fodder grain plus hay production.

The Bighorn Reserve maintains only a minor livestock enterprise. The small community herd is being enlarged by a twenty head governmental rotating herd, but further expansion would necessitate the clearing of substantial areas of land.

In the early 1970s the Stoneys set about planning an agricultural development program for their reserves. This project is known as the STAR-program (for Stoney Tribal Agricultural and Ranching Program) and has been conceptualized around five principles:

a) "Develop our land"
b) "Feed our people"
c) "Train our youth"
d) "Start our ranchers"
e) "Sell our surplus"

First priority is being given to the cattle raising component of this program, and the tribal STAR-Ranch was established as a basic production and training facility. For this purpose the leases of the Crawford and Coppock Ranches (which had been leased out by the Department of Indian Affairs shortly after their acquisition for the reserve in 1946) at the eastern extremity of the main Morley Reserve were terminated in 1976, thus providing the band ranch with a landbase of some 4,450 hectar (11,000 acres). At the same time all leases of reserve lands to non-Indian farmers and ranchers were terminated, for example Begg's Ranch (north of the Ghost Reservoir) and Rabbit Lake land. In 1977 the Stoney tribal administration contracted with Agrisearch Investment Analysis Limited to devise a ranching program for the STAR-Ranch with a five year capital development projection. At that time out of the 4,451,8 hectar an area of 2,023.5 hectar was classified as range, 1,189.8 hectar as bush and waste land, and 728.5 hectar as brush. The remainder, 510 hectar or 11 per cent was cultivated: 170 hectar seeded to grain, 97 hectar seeded to pasture, 154 hectar were to be seeded to pasture, and 89 hectar were summerfallow. The ranch had 361 breeding cows, the herd totalling 980 animals. In their proposal Agriseach recommends only 250 breeding cows with a total herd of 652 head of cattle, for this purpose they include a herd reduction program. When the land was resumed by the Stoneys, the range was in sore need of recovery, having been severely overgrazed by the lessees. Therefore, moderate stocking rates and the implementation of grazing systems were urgent recommendations.

To date, the STAR-Ranch is being operated as a cow-calf operation, but farther reaching implications in terms of training functions and other feedback-effects on the general community have so far not been realized. Starting this year though, the ranch is being increasingly utilized for growing feed for the three bands in order to decrease the livestock owners' dependence on off-reserve sources for winterfeed. Thus about 120 hectar (300 acres) are sown to barley, 60 hectar to oats and another 60 hectar to timothy and alfalfa. To make more land available for cultivation, the ranch's cow herd of 134 head is being moved further west, where an additional 390 hectar (960 acres) parcel of land in the Potts Lake area is being used to pasture them, in conjunction with 518 hectar (1280 acres) of the original STAR-pasture. Grazing systems and conservative stocking rates are both realized. In this recent development the livestock component is being managed largely by the Chiniki Band, whereas the tribal STAR-Ranch is shifting its emphasis to forage production. At present the ranch employs four full-time workers.

Another potentially profitable component of the STAR-program is the eventual capitalization on the tribe's buffalo herd, counting about 150 head. At present these animals are being kept at the Stoney Indian Park, but a game ranching type of enterprise is envisaged for the Broken Leg Lake area.

The Stoneys own a second ranch, named Two Rivers, which they acquired in the late 1970s. Located north of the Ghost Reservoir, it encompasses 1,007 hectar (2,488 acres). It is mainly used for recreational purposes and grazes only rodeo stock.

From the above we can conclude that the Stoneys' rangelands are not utilized to their full capactiy. If the residents wanted to embark on further development projects in livestock economy, a proper range survey basing its data on actual site examinations and considering range condition would be needed, plus a reliable head count of all the horses and cattle roaming the reserve. Part of the range is overgrazed and stocked beyond its capacity, especially easily accessible grasslands surrounding residential areas (for example around Morley townsite). Other parts of the reserve, such as resumed leases are well recovered and hardly utilized at all. The reserve as a whole is likely to be understocked, and the problem is primarily one of distribution of livestock and basic management practices.

The grasslands of the Peigan Reserve are dominated by rough fescue, but as mentioned earlier, show a transition to mixed prairie. Consequently microclimatic conditions and overgrazing easily result in an intrusion of more xeric communities. Based on the Price-report (1967) and cross-checked with the provincial Department of Agriculture and the Agricultural Division, Department of Indian Affairs, Grier and McGregor (1977:6) arrive at a carrying capacity of the land of 10 hectar (25 acres) per animal unit per year. This figure comes close to Elgaard's 9.7 hectar (24 acres) per animal unit per year as an average value for the foothills ranching region, and lies somewhere between the Alberta Department of Lands and Forests suggested stocking rates for the western porcupine grass/wheatgrass prairie (zone 3) with 12 hectar (30 acres)/A.U./a and for the rough fescue prairie (zone 4) with 8 hectar (20.4 acres)/A.U./a. While this figure may be useful as a representative value, planning calls for a more differentiated study of the reserve's range resource, although, due to the more uniform topography, the situation is less complex than on the Stoney Reserves. If we take 10 hectar per head per annum to be a valid figure, the 24,282 hectar (60,000 acres) of rangeland on the Peigan Reserve would have a grazing capacity of over 2,400 animal units. There are no estimates available for increased capacities due to improved range management and husbandry techniques and manipulation of the present vegetation cover. The establishment of tame pastures would meet with much more favourable conditions than on the Stoney Reserves, whereas brush control may be applicable to selected areas. Unbroken arable land is able to sustain another 400 animal units, and there is some potential for the establishment of irrigated pasture along the Oldman River, which could accommodate 200 beasts. Price (1967) and government experts estimate that a satisfactory living could be made on a pasture capacity of 115 animal units. Using this figure as a minimum, the Peigan Reserve (rangeland + unbroken arable land + irrigated pasture) has a possible ranch capacity of twenty-six. 500 additional animals could be accommodated at the Timber Limit, provided that winter grazing would be available elsewhere, possibly on the cultivated land. On the main Peigan Reserve the cultivated land is concentrated in the southwest section, with only small blocks in the northwest and northeast. The rest of the land is used for grazing purposes. Of the 24,282 hectar rangeland almost half are being leased to off-reserve ranchers. Some 8,094 hectar (20,000 acres) in the southeast are used as community pasture; 2,024 hectar (5,000 acres) in the northeast of the reserve make up the band ranch, and the remaining roughly 2,000 hectar (4,900 acres) constitute intrividual ranches operated by band members.

The band ranch (Peigan Developments Co. Ltd) presently owns 650 head of cattle and operates as a cow-calf operation. The cattle remain at the ranch only in winter, using the sheltered river bottom land; the community pasture is grazed during the summer months. The ranch employs a manager and three staff, and so far has not assumed any training or experimental functions. During the interviews those individuals who had an opinion about this matter, expressed some frustration over the lack of feedback of their band ranch with regard to the general community. Especially training and employment of band members were mentioned as desirable functions of such a band enterprise.

On the reserve there are thirty-five Peigan ranchers owning approximately 1,500 head of cattle. These enterprises, too, are cow-calf operations. While the average herd size is small, 40-50 head of cattle, there are some larger owners with about 200 animals. In summer all ranchers graze their cattle on the community pasture - its use is free -, whereas in winter each cattle owner looks after his herd on his own land. As on the Stoney Reserve, no grazing systems are implemented, and no manipulation of the natural vegetation is attempted. Hereford cattle predominate as a breed; there are twenty-four band bulls, which are rented by individuals in spring and summer. Marketing is conducted individually, mainly at Fort Macleod. Overheads are not carried by the band, but by the individual operator. Mutual integration of crop production and livestock economy restricts itself to the grazing of stubble.

Among those interviewed there were four individuals who thought of themselves as full-time ranchers (one farmer/rancher). One owns a large herd of 200 cows and 8 bulls, the other herds count between 25 and 70 head. Because of the presence of so many non-Indian owned cattle of the reserve and the practice of leasing out individual plots, livestock ownership by non-ranchers is less widespread among the Peigan than among the Stoneys. But the Peigan, too, show a strong preference for horses with 41 per cent of the sample owning horses compared to only 17 per cent grazing cattle. The sixty Peigan households sampled own 215 horses (not counting those whose owner did not know their exact number) among them, roughly the same number as those owned by the thirty-two Chiniki households visited. Among the Peigan, too, there is a greater tendency to aim for self-sufficiency than for surplus production. Judging from the sample there is an almost unanimous opposition to a cattle cooperative, while people are generally agreeable (at least in theory) to some kind of range management policy. One band member though brought up the valid point, that there might be a problem of continuity with changes in tribal government (every two years).

The Timber Limit is presently being used for recreation, hunting, grazing leases and some logging. It is not integrated into the ranching economy of the main reserve. The present trend is to terminate the grazing leases and to attempt reforestation; besides, the Peigan expect to receive a twenty-five head herd of buffalo in the near future, which will be kept in this area in a game ranching type of enterprise.

The Peigan do not have a source of continuous income like the Stoneys which they could use to offset their shortage of land and capital. Even if they had one, they might not use the same strategy. But when they received the $ 4 million settlement after the LNID-dispute in June 1981, they initiated a program to boost their ranching economy. Fifty per cent of the settlement (which remarkably never went into the trust fund in Ottawa) were distributed among band members; the other half was turned over to the economic development committee for program development. As a consequence a cow-calf program was introduced. There are, at present, twenty-five individuals who received forty cows. Each year the individuals are expected to repay the economic development committee out of the money received from the sale of calves. In turn, this money can be used to purchase more cattle for others to start a herd. It is too early to draw any conclusion on the success of this project.

5.3.2 Dryland Farming

Limitations imposed by the natural environment all but preclude the cultivation of crops on the Stoney Reserves and create severe restrictions for the Peigan Reserve. Nevertheless dryland agriculture established itself in southern Alberta. Wheat is the principal crop, with oats, barley, rye and flax being the other important crops grown. Some mustard and rape are also being cultivated.

Roughly one-third of the Peigan Reserve (16,188 hectar/40,000 acres) can be classified as arable land. Most of this area is concentrated in the southern central part of the reserve, with some smaller acreages located in the more level parts of the northwest. Of the potentially arable land on the reserve a quarter has not been broken and is still being used for grazing purposes. Over 90 per cent of the band's arable land is being leased to white farmers, there being only one Peigan farmer on the reserve. As a result approximately $ 300,000 of rent money is distributed to land occupants with 20 per cent retained by the band for administration costs. Non-Indian farmers take as profits $ 600,000-800,000 from the reserve without any employment or other benefits for band members being generated. Consequently the Peigan landbase - their largest single non-human resource - is badly under-utilized and does not even come close to producing an income for the tribe comparable to its productive capacity. As it is not planned to break any more land than now in cultivation, those 12,140 hectar (30,000 acres) now under crop could accommodate twenty-five farming units of the minimum size of 485 hectar (1,200 acres), or a band farm could be established.

There are many factors working against the development of a sound farming economy among the Peigan. Limitations imposed by the physical environment have been mostly overcome by the "Green Revolution", although nature still requires great capital investment as well as much circumspection from anyone who farms in this area. Factors such as the uneconomically small size of holdings, the overall lack of capital and the absence of adequate technical training have already been discussed in detail (Chapters 5.2.1.2; 5.2.2.2; 5.2.3) and shall not be repeated here. A final complicating force which must not be overlooked is the fact, that crop raising is utterly alien to Plains Indian culture, much more so than livestock economy. The Blackfoot tribes had a vague tradition of agriculture, but even the memory of it was lost in historical times. Ranching, however, was much more akin to their traditional mode of activities than the "drudgery" involved in cultivating the soil, and this preference persists to the present day. Moreover, the constant demands made on the farmer by the annual cycle of activities - including the summer months with spraying, cultivating the summerfallow and weed control - interfere with the rodeo circuit, sundances and Indian Days many Indians like to attend at different locations throughout this season. In comparison, livestock economy tends to be somewhat more accommodating and flexible.

As a result of all these factors combined there hardly is any active engagement in crop cultivation on the part of the Peigan. The one individual involved in farming cultivates almost 1,660 hectar (4,100 acres), 158 (390) of which he "owns" while he leases approximately 1,497 hectar (3700 acres) from twenty-five other band members on a cash basis. Spring barley is the exclusive crop. Summer fallow is not practised due to erosion hazard. About 120 hectar (300 acres) are under hay, and approximately 130 feeder calves are kept from October to April each year. The farmer receives no financial assistance from the band. The farm in question is a large enterprise, but the odds against staying in the business under reserve conditions - high lease payments, high labour turnover, credit problems - are almost insurmountable.

5.3.3 Irrigation Farming

The bringing of water into Lethbridge through the canals of the Canadian North West Irrigation Company in 1900 was the beginning of extensive irrigation in Alberta. From then on this province has been the leading irrigation province in Canada, well ahead of Saskatchewan and British Columbia. Present projects contain approximately one million acres (404,700 hectar) of irrigable land. The Oldman River Basin (running from the Waterton National Park in the southwest, to as far north as Okotoks, and then narrowing towards the Saskatchewan border as it follows the South Saskatchewan River eastward) accounts for about 63 per cent of the total irrigated area in Alberta. Even though the presently irrigated area only utilizes about 5 per cent of the total land in the basin. Dryland agriculture predominates, making up 87 per cent of the total. About one half of this dryland total is cultivated (especially the north and southeast), while the remainder is grazing (west and south). Of the farmers in the region an estimated 34 per cent are irrigating some or all of their land, averaging about 75 hectar (185 acres) of irrigated land per farm (Marv Anderson and Associates Limited 1978: 13). Due to optimum soil conditions the Lethbridge-Taber area grows the more specialized crops such as corn, sugar beets, and vegetables. In the Lethbridge Northern Irrigation District (LNID) and the Magrath and Raymond areas, grains, forages and sugar beets are grown. The Aetna, Mountain View, Leavitt and United Irrigation Districts south of the Peigan Reserve specialize more in forages, hays, and cereals.

In the light of what was said about dryland farming it is hardly surprising that irrigation agriculture has not been able to establish itself on the Peigan Reserve. Some early attempts were made in 1895 when under the supervision of Indian

Agent Nash an irrigation ditch was dug to bring water from Beaver Creek and the Oldman River a total distance of 5 kilometres (8 miles). The purpose was to improve the reserve's grain crop. This undertaking though seems to have been abandoned soon after as no further mention is made thereof in subsequent agency reports.

Anticipating forthcoming developments in this field, the Peigan contracted with Western Soil and Environmental Services for a land irrigability classification of the main reserve as part of the economic component of the Weasel Valley Water Use Study. The results show that from a purely physical point of view nearly one half of the reserve land is potentially irrigable, the irrigable land comprising portions of land presently under crops as well as range pasture. But even after the physical potential for irrigation has been proven many other questions concerning the reserve's irrigation future remain entirely open. The reserve and its surroundings are generally classed as low priority areas with regard to irrigation, as water is not such a limiting factor in the western portion of the area as it is in the eastern irrigation districts. But presuming the Peigan agree to having the storage facility built on their land, they could well insist on special consideration with regard to water services available to them as part of the deal. Irrigation could do much for the economic viability of the small individual holdings so prevalent among the Peigan. On the other hand irrigation farming generally involves a greater outlay of capital per unit area than dry farming and tends to be more labour intensive than the latter. Both these factors could generate problems for the Peigan agriculturalist. But irrigation farming also offers many opportunities for integrating the livestock economy. A large proportion of all farms in the irrigation districts have substantial cow herds or feeding enterprises. For example, in 1973, about three-quarters of the irrigated farms fed out an average of 176 head per year (ibid.: 53). Irrigated forage and feedgrain production is an integral part of the livestock production system. In addition, sugar beet pulp is utilized by feedlot operators as an additional energy source. While dryland producers derive about an equal percentage of their gross income from both livestock and crop production, irrigation farmers may obtain as much as 60 per cent of their gross income from livestock. The gross value of all livestock production in the region may be as much as ten times that of specialty crops - lending considerable credibility to the argument that livestock is really the most important "specialty crop" in the area. But with regard to its potential establishment on the Peigan Reserve it must also be noted that feedlot operation represents a much more advanced stage of livestock management than cow-calf enterprises.

5.3.4   Forestry

The lumbering business is one of the oldest economic activities on the Stoney and Peigan Reserves (see Chapter 3). The Stoneys started cutting timber as early as 1883 which they sold to the Department of Indian Affairs to be used on other reserves. The Peigan established their own sawmill on their Timber Limit at the turn of the century. There is no record when this tribally owned sawmill shut down, but logging of Douglas-fir and lodgepole pine for saw logs, poles and fence posts continued on an haphazard basis. Before 1963 any Peigan Band member could obtain a permit to cut a specified amount of timber and dispose of it on his own. This was not satisfactory, and in 1963 a logging operation using band funds was set up to stock pile Douglas-fir. Johnson Bros. at Cowley, near Pincher Creek, contracted to purchase the logs. This arrangement lasted for a couple of years. At present a pilot project is in operation (started in 1981), utilizing a portable sawmill and employing six individuals to produce lumber.

The Stoneys had continued to provide lumber mills from off the reserve with logs from their forests. In the late 1960s a mill was established on the reserve by a white entrepreneur, Mel's Lumber and Building Supplies Limited, employing some band members. Then a fall-off in the lumber market made it impossible for the owner to continue. In 1972 the Stoneys set up their own sawmill with old, used machinery in the southern forest area of the reserve. It was subject to frequent breakdowns and was never profitable, but it provided an invaluable training ground for young Stoney employees and taught those running it important technical and business skills in its operation. Finally, in 1977, this old mill was replaced by a new automated mill with a planer unit, established south of Morley beside the CPR mainline.

According to Indian Affairs (1) forest land occupies 52 per cent of the Morley Reserves (main reserve plus Rabbit Lake), while grassland occupies 41 per cent. The remainder is covered by brush, muskeg etc. The forested area can be described in more detail as follows (Campbell 1976: 8):

Table 1:   Description of the Forest Land on the Morley Reserves

	hectar	(acres)	per cent
Softwood	11,158	(27,570)	25
Mixedwood	3,458	(8,544)	7
Hardwood	7,057	(17,483)	16
Clearcut	1,250	(3,089)	3
Burn	258	(638)	1
Total	23,181	(57,279)	52

Lodgepole pine and white spruce account for 60 per cent of the total merchantable volume and 90 per cent of the marketable volume. Hardwood species, primarily trembling aspen, form one-third of the total volume, but have limited marketability. The most productive stands of softwood timber are concentrated in the southern part of the reserve on valley slopes facing north. This concentration can be attributed to the northerly aspect which aids in conserving moisture. The best sites are found on the lower slopes and in the deep soiled portions of drainage channels giving protection from dry chinook winds (see Chapter 5.1.4). The Rabbit Lake Reserve, too, contains sizable stands of merchantable softwood timber according to the same pattern. The southern warm slopes are erosion-prone and should be left undisturbed (Kumar 1976: 6).

Table 2 shows that although the softwood cover type predominates (51 per cent), immature cutting classes 3 and 4 make up 95 per cent of the stocked forest. Also the large area of poplar in cutting class 3 indicates that poplar has taken over on previously logged softwood sites or after forest fires. It is estimated that the Stoney forests can maintain an annual production of at least 2.5 million board feet (bf) of timber, but more intense management could easily double the annual allowable cut. The land added to the reserve in 1968 woud possibly increase the sawtimber cut by 1.5 million bf per year.

These calculations are based on the assumption that the forest is managed on a sustained-yield basis to ensure its ongoing productivity as a renewable resource. The rotation age for sawlogs is, on an average, 100 years for lodgepole pine and 120 years for white spruce and Douglas-fir. This period includes the time required for the natural regeneration of a new stand. Planting immediately after cutting operations could, therefore, reduce the rotation age and increase the annual cutting budget. Scarification of coniferous cut-over areas is imperative to ease natural regeneration by aiding seed germination and plant establishment. Artificial regeneration - either by seeding or planting - is needed in many areas of the Stoney Reserves without an adequate natural seed source.

---

1) In 1964 the Morley Reserves, Nos. 142, 142B, 143 and 144 were surveyed by personnel from the federal forestry service (Bailey 1964) to determine area and location of forest types, to estimate merchantable volume of softwood timber, and to prepare forest management suggestions. In 1973/74 Indian Affairs personnel checked the survey of 1964 as to changes which had occurred primarily in merchantable softwood stands. In 1976 Kumar from Indian Affairs prepared a Forest Management Plan for 142B (Rabbit Lake). The highway land exchange areas from 1968 are not included in these studies; however, forest cover maps by the Alberta Forest Service do include them.

Table 2: Stocked Forest Area in Hectar by Cover Type and Cutting Class (1)
(Indian Affairs 1974, excludes 1968 highway land exchange)

Cover Type/ Cutting Class	2	3	4	5	Total	(per cent)
Softwood	288	3,758	6,697	415	11,158	(51)
Mixedwood	66	2,002	1,333	58	3,458	(16)
Hardwood	193	5,760	1,072	32	7,057	(33)
Total stocked forest land	547	11,520	9,102	505	21,673	
Per cent of total	3	53	42	2	100	

(1) Cutting Classes:
    CC1 - Unstocked forest land (i.e. requires regeneration)
    CC2 - Stands with natural or artificial reproduction established (i.e. young trees)
    CC3 - Polewood stands or advanced young growth without appreciable bf-volume (i.e. immature timber)
    CC4 - Immature stands containing merchantable bf-volume and showing good growth
    CC5 - Mature thrifty stands (i.e. prime sawlogs)
    CC6 - Overmature stands, diseased and poor growth

Merchantability is determined by existing and forseeable market demands. In Alberta the major markets for forest products are for pulpwood, veneer peeler logs, and sawlogs. However, industries utilizing pulpwood and veneer peeler logs are located in the more northerly areas of the province, which leaves sawlogs for lumber as the major forest product in the region of the Stoney Reserves. In addition there are two possible sidelines of production to realize the full commercial potential of the Stoney forests: post-production from small dimension lodgepole pine and Christmas trees from young stands of white spruce and lodgepole pine, and from tops of trees harvested for posts or sawlogs. Christmas tree production was abandoned two years ago as too uneconomical.

The best sawlog cutting chances are found in the pine, pine-spruce, pine-poplar, spruce, and spruce-fir subtypes in cutting class 4. The spruce-poplar 4 and Douglas-fir-poplar 4 strata contain, on the average, approximately only 2,000 fbm of softwood per acre, which is inadequate for continuous efficient forest operations (Bailey 1964: 13). Stands of Douglas-fir in cutting class 4 occupy only 70 hectar (175 acres) or 0.4 per cent of the total stocked forest land. Most such stands border, or are surrounded by, range land and are subject to frequent trespass by livestock trampling and browsing much of the regeneration. The largest marketable volume so far has been concentrated in two groups of subtypes in cutting class 4: uneven-aged lodgepole pine-spruce, lodgepole pine-Douglas-fir, spruce, and spruce-Douglas-fir; and even-aged lodgepole pine and lodgepole pine-aspen. Selective and clearcutting methods for timber removal are respectively applied to the former and latter groups. With regard to lodgepole pine, approximately two-thirds (3,035 hectar/7500 acres) of the sites are too poor to produce sawlog material and are best suited for post and rail production. These poorer sites are concentrated in the northwest corner of the main reserve; the better sites - those capable of producing sawlog material - are located on the valley slopes of the Bow River. An additional 1,833 hectar (4,530 acres) of lodgepole pine occur in association with trembling aspen (poplar). Early logging in immature stands on these areas would encourage prolific aspen suckering. This, in turn, would hinder spruce and other softwood reproduction. A deferral of cutting in lodgepole pine-aspen types until the pine component reaches sawlog size has been necessary to encourage softwood reproduction and to reduce the reproductive ability of trembling aspen. There being no mature stratum of this type, cutting still is being delayed.

The main cutting areas on the Stoney Reserves are located in the Rabbit Lake block, around Chiniki Lake and - since this year - in the Jumping Pound area, acquired in 1968. With regard to harvesting by clearcutting it is recommendable to proceed in alternate horizontal blocks along the contour, with blocks of about 4 hectar (10 acres) in moderately to strongly rolling (15-30 per cent slope) terrain and larger blocks of about 12 hectar (30 acres) in gently rolling (up to 15 per cent slope) areas. This "staggered block" manner is used for many reasons such as ensuring natural reproduction and soil protection (Kumar 1976: 18 ff). On the Stoney Reserves, however, cutting is still practised in irregular patches. As mentioned previously, much of the land is inadequately stocked and not covered by a "normal" forest, composed of even-aged stands a year apart. Consequently, much selective cutting is practised, whereby conifers of economic size with a diameter over 30 centimetres (12 inches) are harvested.

For three years the Stoneys have replanted seedlings in cutover areas. Reserve residents used to collect cones, which were delivered to the Smoky Lake nursery in central Alberta. Seedlings were then taken back to Morley to be replanted. In this manner about 9,000 seedlings have been planted in the Rabbit Lake Reserve, and approximately 25,000 around Chiniki Lake, as well as smaller numbers around the old sawmill site (Jumping Pound block) and in the proximity of the present mill. Naturally these young trees are in constant danger from trespassing livestock, especially the numerous free-roaming horses. This year first attempts are being made to grow seedlings on the reserve, at the sawmill. However, raising of seedlings on large permanent nurseries or the on site temporary nurseries tends to be a very elaborate and expensive affair. A permanent nursery would require sophisticated equipment and qualified manpower. Fencing, water, heating, transplanting, transporting, storing, and protection from fungal diseases and rodents need to be planned. Under these circumstances it is more likely that the Stoneys will continue to rely on a reciprocal arrangement with Alberta Forest Service institutions such as the Smoky Lake nursery, where the seed collection is done by the Stoneys, and the growing stock is provided by the Alberta Forest Service.

From previous experiences it is apparent that in order for a sawmill operation to be economically viable its annual production must amount to 5 million bf per year. Since the prime motive behind the Stoney sawmill is the creation of employment and providing forest products for tribal projects, economic viability is not of paramount importance, and 2 million bf per year is often cited as an acceptable production (Campbell 1976; Underwood McLellan and Associates 1969). At present though, the new sawmill only turns out 0.5 million bf per year, and the main problem behind this low production is surprisingly enough a shortage of log cutters. The mill employs (besides student employment during the summer) a full-time crew of 17 who work alternately at the millsite and in the bush (shutting down the mill). It also employs an off-reserve lumber grader. Nevertheless the sawmill fulfills many purposes for the reserve community. 50-75 per cent of its produce is used on the reserve for housing programs, public buildings such as the Nakoda Lodge, the new restaurant and service station, on ranches, poles for fencing etc. Firewood (softwood) is collected by reserve residents and sold to the sawmill where it is cut into appropriate sizes and sold to Calgary. The mill sells its lumber to ranches, farms and contractors in Cochrane and other localities. Having their own planer, the Stoneys are in a position to sell dressed and graded lumber (1) and, therefore, to derive the maximum profit of a generally high quality product.

Logging operations on the Bighorn Reserve are not integrated with the activities of the Morley sawmill. The Bighorn block contains 1,538 hectar (3,800 acres)

---

1) Many small sawmills sell rough ungraded lumber to other companies who, by dressing and grading, receive the maximum value from the lumber. Dressed lumber is lumber that has been surfaced by a planer to attain smoothness and uniformity of size. Grade stamped lumber (identifies the mill, grade, moisture content and species) is the buyer's assurance that the lumber has been inspected by a qualified and supervised grader, and that the lumber was graded under a grading rule approved by the Canadian Lumber Standards (C.L.S.).

of forest land, of which 1,133 (2,800) support merchantable softwood sawtimber totalling 11.9 million bf. A Rocky Mountain House sawmill, owned by the Fisher Lumber Company, entered into an agreement with the band in 1967-68 to purchase sawlogs from the reserve forest. Initially about 2 million bf of white spruce and lodgepole pine were cut selectively from several stands. Band members were paid for cutting and limbing, and an additional stumpage fee was paid into the band fund. Skidding and hauling was done by Fisher. A small portable sawmill was set up on the reserve, but lack of workers forced it to close in 1968. A forest survey done in 1969 (Bonnor) recommends a continuance of selective cutting of sawlog-size and possibly some degree of diversification by selling waste products to the pulpmill in Hinton. But at present there are no logging activities on the Bighorn Reserve.

5.3.5 Outdoor Recreation

Outdoor recreation is the most recent development of all the activities involving the renewable resource sector on the reserves. Apart from a YMCA-camp that was being run on the reserve on a lease basis and a few Stoneys working as hunting guides, outdoor recreational development was only initiated by the Stoneys after the onset of selfgovernment. It goes without saying that the location of the Morley Reserve midway between Banff National Park and the City of Calgary has a most significant bearing on its potential for outdoor recreation activities. It lies on the threshold of one of the best known and established outdoor wilderness areas in North America. Banff National Park with such well-known attractions as Lake Louise serves as the eastern gateway to a series of national parks, including Jasper National Park, Kootenay National Park and Glacier National Park. Moreover, in this context Banff National Park is of greater significance as an attractor than as a competitor to any commercial recreation facilities that might be developed by the Stoneys. Secondly, the geographic location of the Stoney Reserve relative to the City of Calgary also has important implications. With its phenomenal growth occurring at present, it becomes increasingly difficult to provide the necessary outdoor recreational facilities within its boundaries and on its outskirts. Increasing urbanization of the overall provincial population and a concurrent rise in capital availability and leisure time add to the trend. The recent development of Kananaskis Country as a recreational region bordering on both the Morley Reserve and Eden Valley attested to the need of alleviating congestion in the existing national parks and of providing greater recreational opportunities in the Eastern Slopes.

The Stoneys were aware of this need and also of the great scenic beauty of many parts of their reserve. Therefore, they had a recreation resource study conducted by Underwood McLellan and Associates Limited Consultants in 1969/70. Based on a physical evaluation of the reserves' (Morley proper and Rabbit Lake) resource potential and a market analysis as far as the limited material available permitted it, the consultants prepared a longterm blueprint for recreational projects they deemed feasible for various parts of the reserves. Their suggestions centred around (but were not restricted to) summer recreational activities and included the following:

- a highway commercial area in the southwest at the junction of highways No. 1 and No. 40, comprising a museum, a historical complex, a reconstruction of Fort Peigan, a riding stable, a trailer park, motels, a hotel and restaurant and a buffalo paddock;
- development of facilities around Lake Chief Hector with campground, supper club, cabins, boat docks, riding stable, playground;
- two alternative proposals for the Chiniki Lake area, one featuring developments mainly on the eastern part of the lake with a distinctive lodge and motel, extensive cabin development, teepee village, trailer court, restaurant, riding stables, camping, picnic and boating facilities, and a winter sport area, the second alternative featuring cabin development along the entire south shore of the lake;
- extensive development of the southwest shore of the Ghost Reservoir about four kilometres east of Morley Village with all sorts of boating facilities, beaches, weekend cottages and general recreational areas;
- a dine and dance restaurant on the Transcanada Highway;

- a guest ranch at Potts' Lake;
- less intensive development of the northwestern part of the reserve as a wilderness area catering to picnics, camping and fishing with a hunting lodge, cabins and horse stables on Broken Leg Lake to serve as a base from which the Stoneys can operate a big game guide operation to take advantage of the hunting inherent in the forest lands to the north and west of this part of the reserve;
- establishment of a fishing lodge, cabins, campsites and picnic areas around Rabbit Lake.

Thus the main developmental thrust of these propositions is aimed at the southwest section of the reserve, which in addition to being traversed by the Transcanada Highway and Highway No. 1A is highly scenic foothill country terminating in the Rocky Mountains themselves, and containing attractive lakes and streams. In contrast, the eastern area is relatively treeless, rolling prairie land. The northwestern area and the Rabbit Lake block are at present rather inaccessible due to inadequate road development, hence the less elaborate development proposals.

To date the consultants' development plan has had little impact on the actual happenings on the Stoney Reserve. With a limited landbase at their disposal as it is, and valuing their privacy, the Stoneys are understandably ambivalent about a large scale influx of foreigners in their midst. Chiniki Lake with its picturesque setting and view of the Rocky Mountains and the Kananaskis Valley is regarded by many as the beauty spot of the reserve, and even Bailey's forestry study (1964) proposed developments for golfing, skiing, camping and cottage sites in this area. On the other hand a large segment of the Stoney population is strongly opposed to any development at that place, as the lake has great cultural significance to the Stoney people themselves. Near its western extremity their sundance lodge site is located and used for this purpose every summer.

But, nevertheless, the Stoneys have initiated recreational projects of their own during the last decade. In doing so they are aware that by incorporating their Indian culture and identity in their projects, they have something to offer which cannot be duplicated outside the reserve. Their "Wilderness School" on the shores of Lake Chief Hector which was in operation from 1974 to 1979, illustrates the potential but also the limitations and dangers inherent in such an undertaking. The Wilderness School was basically operated as a summer camp for white teenagers. The Stoneys had a contract with the Society for the Study of the Heritage of Canada who was responsible for marketing the programs and for supplying and transporting a pre-designated number of students to the school, while the Stoneys were responsible for designing, planning and executing all camp programs and activities. These programs and activities centred around material and non-material aspects of Stoney culture, such as general outdoor survival skills, fishing, canoeing, horseback riding, but also natural food identification, handicrafts, music and dance. It was this more intrinsic aspect of Indian culture that raised the concern of many band members. During interviews conducted by one of the band members, Sykes Powderface, on such topics as the Wilderness School and SCEP, he found an astounding lack of information on the school's programs among the reserve population; many associated it with a "dude ranch" concept. Others, however, who were better informed, many elders and politicians among them, expressed bitter criticism especially of the imparting of such knowledge as herbal first aid remedies to non-Indians. The teaching of the practical use of Indian medicine was an infringement of rituals which are highly respected and honored. Their knowledge is considered to be a gift from the Great Spirit, and the question of who is qualified to teach them and to whom knowledge may be imputed is a matter of grave concern lest unforeseen punishment by the Great Spirit may result. A combination of factors such as the above-mentioned, managerial problems and poor public relations resulted in a non-renewal of a second five-year contract between the Stoneys and the Heritage Society, with the Wilderness School closing down in 1979.

The location of its base camp on the edge of Lake Chief Hector is now being occupied by the beautiful log structure of the Nakoda (1) Institute, opened in June 1981. The Nakoda Institute is a brainchild of Chief John Snow of the Wesley Band. It is an educational-spiritual centre with a variety of functions; it houses the Stoneys' cultural centre, is rented out for such different purposes as a hide-tanning seminar for Stoney women, church group meetings, Indian organization meetings, workshops and much more. Thus the Stoneys use the facilities for their own purposes, and in addition the institute brings in revenue from outside the reserve. For the future they plan vocational courses at this centre, and eventually they would like Nakoda to be a yearround educational facility with ties to other major educational institutions in the province. There is already a residence, capable of accommodating up to thirty people, but plans call for more sleeping accommodations.

Some "Indian flair" is also exhibited by another project of the Stoneys, actually the first recreational enterprise they embarked upon: the Stoney Indian Park. It was conceived and developed in 1970 as a campground and recreational area comprising approximately 520 hectar (1,280 acres) and located about 13 kilometres (8 miles) west of Morley close to Highway No. 1A, overlooking the Bow River Valley. Only about 20 per cent of the area is being used for camping facilities; the remainder is taken up by the buffalo paddock and open area. Camping facilities provided include water, washrooms, a cookhouse, picnic tables and parking space. An original element of the Indian Park is a teepee village. It was originally established in 1970 as a show place for tourists and campers, with some pole and moss and spruce bark teepees. Then, in 1973, canvas teepees were purchased for the annual Indian Ecumenical Conference (2), which can be rented for a nightly charge during the summer season. A final element was a riding stable, which was discontinued though in 1978. The Stoney Indian Park employs two gatemen and two maintenance men. Despite its obvious potential it seems to suffer from lack of promotion. During the author's sporadic visits on weekends during the season (June-September) only few visitors were encountered, although there is a capacity of over 200 camp sites. According to the campground superviser (John Poucette, pers.comm.) an average summer weekend would have about 20-25 campers, but there could be as many as 50-60 on certain holidays. People usually come to enjoy the scenery, watch the buffalo (if within sight) or to go fishing, although at present there are no guides or supervisers on the grounds. Among the more regular customers are boy scouts, church groups and trailer groups. Apparently the band council has also been approached by a skidoo-club and a cross country skiclub (Calgary-based) to make facilities available during the winter season, but the Stoneys declined.

The Peigan Reserve's potential for recreational and tourism development is more limited, and at present the Peigan are not deriving any income from this source. But the reserve is located on the only major southern Alberta east-west highway route between the Transcanada Highway to the north and the United States border. The No. 3 Highway which bisects the reserve leads to such tourist attractions as the Crowsnest Pass area and Waterton Lakes National Park, and there is some limited potential for the Peigan to take advantage of the tourist traffic passing through by means of a roadside camp or picnic ground.

However, the Head-Smashed-In buffalo jump just outside the northern periphery of the reserve on secondary road No. 516 could turn out to be a particular attraction. This site is the oldest and largest buffalo jump on the Canadian prairie.

---

1) The name "Nakoda" comes from the Stoney word for Sioux, of whom the Stoney are a part, and architecturally the structure is reminiscent of a teepee, with its main hall being centred around a large fireplace, and each of the three main meeting rooms upstairs being shaped like a teepee, with the cedar siding coming together in a V at the peak of each room.
2) The Indian Ecumenical Conference is an event which draws thousands of Indian people from all parts of North America to Morley each summer. The idea of an Indian Ecumenical Conference to revive the native religion was born in the late 1960s, and the first one was held in the summer of 1970 at the Crow Agency, Montana. The second conference took place at the Stoney Indian Park in 1971, and the Stoneys have hosted the event ever since.

At the base of the cliff is an 11 meter thick layer (about 60 by 240 meters) of bones of buffalo killed from about 3700 B.C. to the early 19th century. The jump is a provincial historic site, and Alberta Culture is currently working on plans to develop the site in a way that will allow maximum access for the public consistent with the aim of long-term preservation. There is a good chance that the Peigan will be able to participate in this development.

Moreover use could be made of scenic areas along the Oldman River. The Canada Land Inventory for outdoor recreation (Lethbridge 82H) rates the area as class 2 to 3, high to moderately high, and the Oldman River is very attractive for canoeing. The Peigan themselves use the river bottom land quite extensively for fishing, weekend picnics etc., and there is a good potential for camping. If however a dam is constructed at the Brocket site, there will be considerable adverse impact on this recreational potential, and it is questionable to what degree the reservoir itself would lend itself to water-based recreation, depending on water level fluctuations, creation of mud flats, and the steepness and stability of adjacent shoreland.

Finally, the Peigan have their Timber Limit, an attractive piece of land in the Porcupine Hills. In 1975 they hired Synergy West Limited Consultants to investigate landuse alternatives for this area, and a preliminary assessment narrowed the range of possibilities to
a) an education/recreation centre,
b) a guest ranch,
c) a commercial campground,
d) a game ranch,
e) cattle grazing, and
f) a recreation subdivision.

The consultants came to the conclusion that the concept of a recreation subdivision of 200 to 400 cottage lots enhanced by facilities such as a lodge and recreation centre would have the greatest potential of any alternative in terms of economic returns, employment opportunities and skills development, with the other recreational options (a to c) not being economically viable. They suggested a strong preservationist ethic as basis for the development, realized by sensitive road construction and building standards and by preserving large parcels of land in a natural state. A preliminary market analysis indicated that approximately 200 purchasers could be attracted to the subject property; a lease term of 40 years was recommended. To date there is no indication that the Peigan Band Council has any intention to follow these suggestions. Their present priority is reforestation of the area.

Thus neither of the two reserves has been penetrated by the secondary home market, although the Stoney and Peigan lands both offer considerable potential for it with regard to access and distance from larger population centres, site factors and opportunities for recreational activities. It is a major decision for an Indian community to bring significant numbers of non-Indians onto the reserve for short periods of time, let alone having outside people actually constructing their own homes upon reserve land. Even the concept of leasing land for 20 or 40 years may appear to Indian people like giving up the land. That it can work - provided that it is clearly understood that ownership, control and management of the land remain with the tribe, while jobs and income are created - is shown by two other southern Albertan reserves. One example is the Siksika Cottage Resort on the Blackfoot Reserve at Gleichen, a 131 hectar (324 acres) holiday resort with 366 lots and recreational facilities such as a club house, a man-made lake, a convenience store, three paved tennis courts, a golf course and rental horses. The second example is provided by the Sarcee Band, southwest of the Calgary city limits. Their Redwood Meadows project presents a somewhat different situation as it is a real estate enterprise which allows building on parcels of reserve land leased for 99 years. Just recently the Alberta Court of Appeal has ruled that provincial laws do not apply to non-Indian housing developments located on Indian reserves; as a consequence the hundred families of Redwood Meadows do not have the right to form a municipal government and to pay school and property taxes: They must negotiate with the province for services like education and busing grants that go automatically to other Alberta communities.

5.4 The non-renewable Resource Sector: Potential and economic Activities

The Stoney Reserves are underlain by substantial natural gas reserves, distributed in several fields (see Chapter 5.1.5). During the last decade royalties from this resource have contributed to a considerable rise in the Stoneys' standard of living. John Snow (1977: 141) points out a striking analogy when he says: "We do not see a difference between the gas and the buffalo. It is all part of our world. As we once were helped by the buffalo and used them wisely, so we can now be helped by the gas, if we use it wisely." Just as the buffalo was the staff of life in their traditional subsistence, the gas has eased their transition into modern times. Both are considered gifts of the land they are living on.

An amendment to the Indian Act in 1919 made it possible to exploit minerals on Indian reserves without the land being surrendered by the band in question. Although minerals (including fossil fuels) were considered as belonging to the provinces, prior to this amendment no lease of surface rights for the purpose of taking out these minerals could be given without a surrender thereof from the band. The original reason for the passage of this amendment was as follows: "Owing to local conditions, misapprehension or hostility on the part of a band, it is not always possible to secure a surrender for mining rights. This obstacle has been effectively overcome by the amendment" (Indian Affairs Annual Report 1919: 30). Though not intended, it has also enabled Indian bands to strike a more lucrative deal about a share in the profits of the resource with the party acquiring a working interest.

Nevertheless Indians have bitter complaints about the federal government's handling of their money. Resource companies send royalty and lease payments directly to the Department of Indian Affairs, which then deposits the money into the Trust Fund. According to Charles Wood, head of the national Council of Chiefs, the bands are paying dearly in lost interest dollars for the government's bureaucratic delays in depositing payments in the trust account (Kainai New 1981, Oct. No. 2). The oil and gas resources of Indian lands are developed by oil companies under the Indian Oil and Gas Regulations. Permit and lease parcels are offered for public tender and the rights are granted for the highest cash bonuses. The Stoneys retain control over the routing of pipelines and the position of gas wells, taking care that service corridors are established within existing cutlines and other disturbed areas.

One of the larger gas fields the Stoneys are deriving a profit from is the Jumping Pound West Field. It contains three pools, A, B and C, which are unitized: Pools A and B are included in Unit 1 and pool C is included in Unit 2. Both units are operated by Shell and the gas is processed in the Jumping Pound Gas Plant. The Stoneys have a royalty on 25 per cent of the production from Unit 1 and on 33 per cent of the production from Unit 2 (1). Although their interest is higher in Unit 2, they are obtaining more revenue from Unit 1 since the pool is considerably larger and is produced at nearly three times the rate. The Stoneys have the option of taking their royalty share in dollar, as they are at the present time, or taking it in kind and processing their own gas. In 1974 D & S Petroleum Consultants Limited advised the Stoneys that it was not economic for them to build their own gas plant since it would cost less to process gas through the Shell plant. The situation should be re-evaluated though if additional reserves are discovered in the area and a new plant is required to process the newly discovered gas.

This need did arise in the mid-1970s for gas reserves found immediately north of Morley and some 10 kilometres (6 miles) further northwest along the Ghost River, which are being exploited by PanCanadian Petroleum Limited and Phillips Petroleum Canada Limited. There is no reserve capacity at either the Wildcat Hills Plant (the

---

1) The Stoneys participate in 6 tracts within Unit 1 which have a total tract factor or participation in the unit of 25.1659 per cent, and they share in 4 tracts within Unit 2, which have a total participation factor of 33.2864 per cent.

closest) or the Jumping Pound Plant. A number of potential plant sites and pipeline routes were investigated with regard to their impact on the physical, biological and cultural environment. Three of the five potential sites were located on the Morley Reserve. The first choice after the site selection study in the summer of 1975 - a site west of Morley - was deemed unacceptable, however, after consultation with the Stoney Band Council, because it would interfere with the potential of the area for motion pictures. As a result, another more northerly on-reserve site was chosen and the PanCanadian Petroleum Limited Morley Gas Plant established. The primary effect of the establishment of a plant on the reserve is creation of employment during the construction phase and revenues in respect of surface land usage for the plant, access roads and pipelines.

The PanCanadian Morley Plant went into operation in July 1980. As was previously mentioned, the Morley plant site was originally selected as the preferred site for processing of both Morley and Ghost field gas. The present plant site has sufficient space for a single large plant with capacity for both gas fields or for two separate plants. However, the PanCanadian plant was designed to handle Morley gas only (the Stoneys receive a 52 per cent royalty) and does not have excess capacity to process Ghost gas. As a consequence need for yet another plant was soon apparent. This project was proposed by Phillips Petroleum Company Western Hemisphere and partners. A total of eleven potential gas plant locations were identified and evaluated; three of these were identified as preferred gas processing locations and subjected to a comparative environmental impact assessment. One of these locations is next to the existing PanCanadian plant. If this site were selected, Phillips would probably have to construct a totally independent gas plant but could share such facilities as roads, treatment ponds, water supply facilities and sales gas pipelines. Benefits to the Stoneys would be the same as those derived from the PanCanadian plant: surface leases and the equivalent of what Phillips would otherwise be required to pay in respect of industrial facility municipal taxes. The new plant might also provide employment opportunities for local residents (long-term rather than only construction jobs), and Phillips is considering the establishment of training programs which might enhance the local benefit.

The second potential site is located on Crown land that was transferred by the Provincial Crown to the administration of the Federal Crown, in return for the Transcanada Highway right-of-way through the Stoney Reserve (see Chapter 5.2.1.1). The Stoneys have to date not accepted the transferred land for incorporation as part of the reserve due to the fact that the land proposed for transfer did not include mines and minerals, thus barring the Indians from participating in the Ghost field. Consequently, the land continues to be administered as Federal Crown land. Under these circumstances the Stoneys would not receive any revenues from facilities established on those lands, as all revenues would go directly to the General Revenues of Canada. The Department of Indian Affairs would probably not issue leases on the Federal Crown land without consent of the Stoney Band Council, which they are not likely to give. This situation could change, if the mineral rights conflict were resolved or if at any time the Stoneys should decide to accept the transferred land as reserve land.

Should the plant be located on the third potential site (on private land), little or no benefits would accrue to the Stoneys. At present (Summer 1982) the question still has not been decided upon.

Apart from occasional exploration leases, the Peigan are not deriving any income from fossil fuels. Due to the complex geology of the area intensive exploration is needed to locate reserves. Exploration leases were held in 1966/67, and again in 1979/80.

But even this chance has been seriously curtailed by a recent provincial government decision (June 1981) that oil companies exploring on Indian reserves will no longer be eligible for provincial incentive payments. These incentives took the form of a credit against royalty and lease payments to the province. About 35 per cent of the cost of drilling higher-risk wells could be subtracted from bills owing the provincial treasury. Not surprisingly the first auction of exploration permits on

Indian lands since this ruling and the introduction of the National Energy Program showed a drastic decline in April 1982. Alberta bands collected only $ 503,000 from the sale of oil and gas exploration permits. Although 84 parcels of Indian land were offered, only 17 bids were accepted. In comparison, Alberta reserves earned $ 26.8 million from the sale of permits in the nine months preceeding the October 1980 federal budget.

Chapter 6

Settlement Pattern and Communication Network

The Stoney and the Peigan Reserves are both characterized by a dispersed settlement pattern, with a concentration of part of the population at two townsites, Morley and Brocket. These two townsites or villages, as they are also called, accommodate about 2 per cent of the Stoney and 25 per cent of the Peigan residences; in addition, they offer certain central goods and services to the reserve communities and serve as administrative centres. In both cases the townsites were not the original population concentrations on the reserves. The historical Morleyville Settlement was just to the east of Morley Townsite on the northern Bow River bank, where the basements of the 1875 Methodist church and some other buildings are still visible, and where there is today a replica of the old church, marked as a provincial historical site. The focus of settlement was shifted to the west when the Indian agency was established at this location. On the Peigan Reserve the first Indian agency was in the northern part of the reserve, at the confluence of the Oldman River and Olsen Creek. The site of Brocket was established with the construction of the Crowsnest Pass railway in 1900, but it was not before the 1950s that the Peigan people started moving there, followed by such facilities as their schools and churches.

Both communities are spread out with Brocket in particular (due to its greater number of private homes) having a somewhat scattered lay-out. Architecturally the public buildings in Brocket are characterized by a plain modernistic style, whereas in Morley one notes a distinct (and successful) effort to exhibit originality. This difference is less an expression of different taste than a reflection of the differing financial situation of both tribes. In Morley the progress of band administration buildings is almost symbolic: Up to 1969 the small white post office and agency building was the meeting place for the Stoney Band Council. By the time self-government was restored to the Stoneys in 1969, band affairs were administered from a stylized teepee building. By 1978 band operations required even more space, and a new, prestigious three million dollar administration complex was constructed.

While Brocket and Morley provide some focal point on the reserves, the majority of the Peigan and Stoney population is scattered in a random manner throughout the reserves. The Stoneys are dispersed quite widely over the main reserve (Rabbit Lake being uninhabited) with some orientation toward the Transcanada and No. 1A highways. The residences of family groupings are about 1 to 1.5 kilometres apart and located on acreages or parcels of land of various sizes (see Chapter 5.2.1.2). Most of the Chiniki and Bearspaw band members live south of the Bow River (with 350 members or 43 per cent of the Bearspaw living on the Eden Valley Reserve), while the Wesley Band occupies land north of the Bow and west of Morley (with 96 band members or 13 per cent residing on the Bighorn Reserve).

One can still find many relics of early settlement on the reserve. The first cabins built by the Stoneys shortly after the treaty were small log structures, with roofs of logs and an outer covering of sod. Each had a mud fireplace and most had mud floors. Originally, many lacked window sashes but had parflech (translucent rawhide) stretched over the openings. Over the decades improvements were made. Plank and shingle roofs replaced the sod, window frames were added along with plank flooring, and proper plaster replaced the mud used to seal the chinks between the logs. Wooden cabins were the only type of accommodation available on the reserve until the late 1960s. It was not before 1968 that the first modern houses were constructed, the first homes on the reserve to have central heating, running water, and indoor plumbing. Electricity had been installed to most homes in 1967 (Snow 1977: 113). The telephone line was not to reach the reserve until 1971, about the same time that indoor plumbing became more common. Nowadays there are virtually no houses without electricity and indoor plumbing. Within the last ten years there also has been a drastic switch from using wood for fuel (94 per cent of all dwellings in 1969, acc. to Underwood McLellan and Associates 1969: 75) to the usage of oil (virtually 100 per cent today).

Twenty new houses are built annually (by about six different outside contractors), and an extensive renovation program is in operation. Today all houses have concrete basements or are set on concrete blocks. The more recently constructed ones are of two main types: either of wooden framed stucco or a modern loghouse (the latter was recently discontinued). Also within the vicinity of many houses a teepee is located, serving as an airy and comfortable accommodation during the summer months. Each house is owned and built by the band and assigned to each family (free of charge). Usually, when a son marries, he requests that a house be built for him near his parents' home, and if the budget provides for it, this is done. Despite the major thrust towards housing development since the onset of self-government the housing situation still appears to be critical as illustrated by the large number of homes that have to accommodate more than one family (see Chapter 5.2.2.1). When young people marry, they usually have to spend the first years of their married life with one or the other set of in-laws. About one-third of the household heads interviewed among the Chiniki expressed dissatisfaction with their accommodation, mostly due to crowded conditions, and secondly due to poor state of repair of the houses.

On the Peigan Reserve the residences are equally scattered, but two general areas can be distinguished: One is between the Oldman River and Highway No. 3 in the north; the other concentration of houses is south of Brocket. The various bands within the tribe show no residential affiliation. The introduction of modern facilities among the Peigan is as recent as with the Stoneys: electricity in the early 1960s, indoor plumbing and central heating (today natural gas) a few years later, and telephone only in 1974. Today 95-98 per cent of the houses have electricity, 60 per cent have complete plumbing, 10 per cent part plumbing while the remainder depends on pumped-in water. One or two per cent still utilize woodstoves - some by choice - while the vast majority switched to natural gas.

Housing shortage is acute. There is an immediate need for 70 new residences - either as replacement for old ones or for new families - a need that is not likely to be satisfied before 1987. At the same time there are 130-140 applications for new accommodation. The annual number of newly built houses fluctuates. While there were 35 in 1981, no funds whatsoever were allocated to housing for this fiscal year, and only Peigan persistence managed to secure funds for 15 new residences. The allocation of new houses to successful applicants is done on the basis of need by a housing committee and subject to council's approval. To finance new houses, the tribe depends on an Indian Affairs subsidy of $ 18,000 per house, the Canada Mortgage and Housing Corporation (CMHC) Low Income Housing programs and loans. Band members pay "rent to own" over 35 years (with CMHC-mortgage subsidies). Before 1976, when means were even more restricted, all houses were built by the band itself. Nowadays bids go out for public tender. While usually 5-6 contractors are involved, many contracts are secured by Kainai Industries Limited, a Blood-owned home-building company. Despite the crowded conditions (see Chapter 5.2.2.1) and other shortcomings, only 22 per cent of the household heads interviewed expressed acute dissatisfaction with the state of affairs which tells us much about the low standards the Peigan are accustomed to. Although new homes are much in evidence on the reserve today, many young working couples or single people are virtually unable to invest in homes for their future.

This dismal housing situation applies to Alberta's Indians in general. The latest housing data as of 1977 (Siggner and Locatelli 1980: 41) indicate that 37 per cent of Indian reserve and settlement houses in Alberta were in need of major repairs or replacement. While the majority of Indian homes had electricity (94 per cent) only 54 per cent had potable water piped into homes and only 48 per cent had sewage disposal and indoor plumbing. These conditions are particularly marked in rural and remote (often northern) communities. By contrast, the 1977 Housing Facilities and Equipment Survey indicated that at least 97 per cent of all houses in the province were equipped with electricity, sewage disposal, indoor plumbing and running water. In Indian homes the lack of facilities is combined with the fact that 39 per cent of the units accommodate two or more families living within or require an addition to accommodate large families. Such overcrowding leads to greatly increased chances of family break-up, poor school grades (no room to study), and the rapid transmission of disease between family members. The demand for housing is bound to increase if we look at the large increase in the principal family-formation age group (20-29 years; see Chapter 5.2.2.1). Nevertheless, in Alberta the federal allocation for Indian housing has been reduced from $ 10.2 million to $ 6 million, while there is a backlog of 826 new houses and 1,574 are in need of major renovations (Kainai News May No. 1, 1982). In 1974 a Central Mortgage and Housing Corporation program was announced which would provide 75 per cent of the funding for 50,000 housing units in rural and small communities over five years if the province would provide the remaining 25 per cent. Purchase of new units was adapted to the income of the prospective owner, similar to other public housing programs. This program, however, did not include registered Indians. The current Indian Affairs housing policy for Indians living on reserves combines the resources of the department, Canada Mortgage and Housing Corporation, and Indian individuals and bands, whose contributions may be in cash and/or labour. The Indian On-Reserve Housing Program enables Indians living on reserves to apply for a ministerial guarantee of a housing loan from the Canada Mortgage and Housing Corporation. The program also provides bands with loans from CMHC or approved lenders as defined in the National Housing Act for low-income rental housing projects on reserves. Only 7 of Alberta's 42 bands make use of special low interest loans. Most reserves depend simply on a $ 22,000-per house Indian Affairs subsidy for building materials and then hire local workers under a federal employment grant.

Road access to both reserves is excellent with principal (allweather) highways running though them: the Transcanada and the provincial Highway No. 1A through the Morley Reserve, and Highway No. 3 through the Peigan Reserve. The Bighorn Reserve is bounded by the David Thompson Highway, and Eden Valley is situated on secondary road No. 541 which is graded and gravelled. Maintenance of the local roads on all reserves though presents problems. As evidenced by the distribution of residences there has been no controlled development or planning with regard to housing location. People were free to locate wherever they desired, thus accounting for the dispersed settlement pattern. It reflects a cultural attitude of pronounced individualism and a dislike of population concentrations. Naturally this factor results in considerable road construction and maintenance costs and creates problems with installation of public services such as sewer and water. Generally access to the residences is quite good, with an increasing number of roads being gravelled and maintained in good condition (band employment programs). But there are a number of houses on both reserves which are only accessible by tracks or trails; other areas where travel is easy enough under dry conditions become all but inaccessible when there is rain or snow. Many Stoney and Peigan children miss a good part of their school year because the school buses simply cannot travel on the reserve roads. Reserve areas which are uninhabited are usually characterized by poor accessibility. There is only a dirtroad leading into the Peigan Timber Limit, which deteriorates the further one drives into the area. The northwestern portion of the Morley Reserve, around Broken Leg Lake, is also uninhabited and only penetrated by trails. Rabbit Lake has no settlement either and is dissected by two roads. The road in the eastern portion (where there are gas wells) is graded and gravelled, whereas the road in the western portion along Rabbit Lake is merely graded. Poor accessibility of these areas tends to affect resource management fields such as forestry and recreational developments.

Chapter 7

The Manufacturing and Servicing Sector

7.1 Secondary Industries

Activities evolving from the land-based economy - be it agriculture, forestry, outdoor recreation or mineral extraction - can still be interpreted as having some degree of continuity from the Indians' traditional mode of economy. The land as provider is a familiar concept to the Indian of old and new times alike.

In contrast, the idea of manufacturing goods for a market rather than just satisfying personal subsistence needs was an alien one. Taking this factor into account plus the problems connected with labour and capital it is hardly surprising that secondary industries established themselves among the Peigan and Stoneys only recently and on a small scale.

A business on a reserve, like any other business, may take the legal form of a single proprietorship, a partnership, a cooperative or a company. Band members can obtain rights to use particular portions of reserve land and can use them for business purposes. If a single proprietor is a band member or if all the members of a partnership are band members, then the business can be located on allotted reserve land without the need for a surrender, a permit or a locatee lease. If a single proprietor is not a band member, if a partnership contains one or more partners who are not band members, or if a business is incorporated, then the business cannot be located on the reserve unless the procedures are followed which allow non-Indians to occupy reserve lands. The tax exemptions stipulated in the Indian Act apply only to Indian individuals. Companies have no income tax exemption simply because they are located on Indian reserve land. If a business is incorporated, it is not an Indian within the meaning of the Indian Act, although any shareholders and employees who are Indians may have a tax exemption on dividends and salaries. The business itself will only be tax exempt if it is a single proprietorship run by an Indian or a partnership, all members of which are Indian. There is an alternative way of establishing an enterprise on reserve land (chosen by the Stoneys). Some small scale industry (or a band farm or sawmill) could simply be located on band land (unallotted reserve land) and run by the band. Strictly, no legal entity would be involved since bands are generally not considered legal entities. There would be no limited liability and the tax status of the band would be uncertain.

On the Peigan Reserve there are two manufacturing enterprises, both located in Brocket: Pe-Kun-Nee Garments Ltd. and Peigan Crafts Ltd. Since 1973, Pe-Kun-Nee Garments Ltd. has grown from a six-employee shop doing contract work for the government to a factory employing more than fifty people and manufacturing three full lines of cover-alls, as well as a variety of custom garments and jeans. At present the enterprise mainly serves the western Canadian market, but the company plans to enter the northwest United States market. The second Peigan industrial enterprise, Peigan Crafts Ltd., manufactures moccasins. It is a split cow-hide moccasin with sheep skin lining and rabbit fur trim; ironically the rabbit fur must be imported from Europe, while the sheep skin comes from Ontario and the cowhide is supplied from Alberta. Peigan Crafts Ltd. has about 140 established retail outlets and 89 seasonal outlets scattered throughout British Columbia and Alberta. A new account was recently opened in Anchorage, Alaska, and orders were also received from Belgium, West Germany and Australia. Plans are underway to boost production by introducing two shifts. The first shift of 23 employees will work form 7 a.m. to 3 p.m. and the second shift from 3 p.m. to 11 p.m. Negotiations are underway to establish retail outlets in southern Ontario, and there are also plans for experimentation in other provinces and the northern states. An introduction of informal work patterns or flexible shifts has not been attempted by the Peigan. For the near future the construction of a new industrial complex is planned to house Peigan Crafts Ltd. and Pe-Kun-Nee Garments Ltd. which is now located in the old school building. An increase of production, addition of new product lines, the establishment of a retail store, laundry facility and restaurant are to accompany this move. In addition to these factories there is a small handicraft operation, a family enterprise where production takes place in homework and the products are marketed in a small store on Highway No. 3 where it enters Brocket. Another private enterprise, a jewelery and confections store opened in Brocket in June 1982. While the two factories offer employment and skill development to a great number of women, there unfortunately is no similar long term employment industry for men.

On the Stoney Reserves handicraft production is the only secondary industry in operation. This tribal enterprise came into being in 1970 and moved to a new and conveniently located (on N-Morley Road, connecting Highways No.'s 1 und 1A) building in 1979. Stoney Handicrafts employs a manager and ten workers who engage mainly in the production of moccasins. In addition, about fifty reserve residents produce a variety of objects in homework (supplying their own material) and sell them to the shop. The number of Stoneys involved in commercial handicraft production has sharply declined in recent years (from over 100) after the per capita royalty payments set in; at the same time purchase from and trade with other Indian groups in Canada and the United States, who use the shop as a retail outlet, are on the increase. Trade is carried on with native people from as far away as Arizona and the Yukon.

7.2 Service Industries

Morley and Brocket constitute focal points of the reserves and provide certain goods and services for their hinterland. But upon closer investigation it becomes evident that they fulfill this function only to a rather limited degree.

In Brocket there are two service industries: a grocery store and a service station. The Crowlodge Grocery Store is privately owned by a band member and was opened in October 1980. A number of supporting agencies such as the Federal Business Development Bank, the Indian Equity Foundation and the Department of Indian Affairs made this project possible. "Ed's Service Station" is located on the No. 3 Highway and opened in 1981. It has two fuel pumps and also deals in automotive parts, accessories and tires.

Besides these service industries there are a few institutions catering to the band's recreational needs. The Crowlodge complex (administration building) contains an indoor hockey rink. A new community centre - built with the help of money received for oil and gas exploration leases - was opened in 1981. It includes a gymnasium with a seating capacity of 300 in addition to a poolroom, showers, locker rooms, the recreation administration offices and a drop-in centre with kitchen. It will not only accommodate sports functions but also band meetings and social events such as pow wows, A.A.-meetings, Societies' meetings etc. The upper level will house tribal research, recreation, Native Outreach, alcohol services and a life skills and upgrading class. The Oldman River Cultural Centre houses the Peigan's archives, cultural resource material and caters to such functions as weekly elders' get-togethers or youth wilderness camps. There is no doctor or nurse on the reserve. The health centre merely provides instruction in hygiene and related matters by community health and childcare workers. A daycare centre is located in the administration complex. Thus it is obvious that the Peigan have to satisfy many of their needs off-reserve. Recreational facilities - a decade ago virtually non-existant - have been considerably improved, especially with the construction of the new multipurpose community hall. But the Peigan still leave their reserve to do literally all their shopping. People interviewed generally complained about high prices and limited stock of the on-reserve grocery store. Reserve residents do most of their shopping for day-to-day needs at the Pincher Creek Co-op, with fewer families going to Fort Macleod or Lethbridge on a regular basis. More specialized and infrequently required goods such as clothing are usually purchased in Lethbridge. People generally seem to be quite satisfied to travel to these neighbouring centres for their requirements, and only very few individuals saw a need for a major shopping facility in the community of Brocket. On the other hand, such basic service facility as a public laundromat is sorely missed by almost every household.

The situation among the Stoneys is not too different. The only grocery store on the reserve is the so-called Stoney Trading Post, built in 1961 and owned and operated by non-Indians. It is frequented mostly by young people, and also sells gas. The Stoneys do most of their shopping at the Calgary Co-op, with only a few families visiting Cochrane or Canmore for this purpose. Many of the Chiniki Band members interviewed thought it desirable to establish in Morley a band enterprise comparable to the Co-op store. There are two band-owned service stations on the Morley Reserve. The older one, established in 1974, is situated on the No. 1A Highway at the turn-off to the Stoney Indian Park. It caters to reserve residents and travellers passing through alike, selling confectionary staples to its customers. The second service station just opened in 1982 and is located on the Transcanada Highway, at the Morley turn-off, adjacent to the new Chief Chiniki Restaurant. This 55-seat restaurant which opened in summer 1981 was an idea of Chief Frank Powderface of the Chiniki Band and is to commemorate Chief John Chiniki, one of the three Stoney Chiefs who signed Treaty Seven. The beautiful log structure is situated on top of a rise which offers a commanding view of the mountains and foothills. A special feature of this restaurant is that it does not merely offer traditional North American cuisine, but a variety of native dishes such as venison, fish and meat of buffalo raised on the reserve, all served with bannock.

The Morley townsite contains a band hall, a multi-purpose recreation complex with a gymnasium, a swimming pool, a hockey arena and a drop-in centre, a daycare centre and a health centre. The latter is administered from the Foothills Hospital in Calgary and offers somewhat more comprehensive services than the one in Brocket. A doctor is in the clinic from 9 a.m. to 5 p.m. five days a week, in addition to interns and residents from the Foothills Hospital. There are two registered nurses, a community health worker and a childcare worker.

We can conclude with regard to both communities, Peigan and Stoneys, that their degree of "institutional completeness" is low. According to CUTIA (Calgary Urban Treaty Indian Alliance, no date, p. 5),

> All ethnic groups seek institutional completeness because it makes it easier for them to have their needs met in terms of a common language, unique cultural modes of behaviour and expression, and more general acceptance and self-confidence to deal within one's own social-cultural milieu. Institutional completeness strives toward providing all the needs within the group.

The Stoneys and Peigan must depend for many of their needs on the larger society. Morley provides its reserve hinterland with a slightly wider range of services than does Brocket, while the Peigan are geographically closer to off-reserve communities than the Stoneys.

Chapter 8

Conclusion and Outlook:

The Peigan and Stoney Reserves as "underdeveloped" Areas and "internal Colonies"

The previous chapters have introduced two reserves which illustrate the development problems of Canada's native population. These reserves differ culturally, economically and physically. As members of the Sioux and Blackfoot Nations respectively, the Stoneys and the Peigan are culturally distinct. Even today the Stoneys remain more secluded and self-contained than the Blackfoot tribes in comparison, while at the same time assuming an important role in Indian cultural revival as annual hosts of the Indian Ecumenical Conference.

In terms of natural resources the Peigan Reserve's main assets are its good agricultural and grazing land and its location on the Oldman River, a water body of vital importance for irrigation purposes. For this reason the Peigan have recently put up a strong stand in negotiations concerning land and particularly water, because these are the only potential sources for a much needed economic boost. The Stoney Reserve has a distinct potential for livestock economy, forestry and recreation, but its mainstay is a non-renewable resource, natural gas, which has had a major impact on all other sectors of the reserve's economy.

Like the buffalo of old gas has helped the Stoneys in a variety of ways, but unlike its predecessor it has not been able to provide its beneficiaries with that wholesome way of life which satisfies not only a people's economic needs but also its social and spiritual needs. The Stoneys are plagued with the same social problems as all the other tribes. Another difference is equally important: As a non-renewable resource gas is finite, and one has to ask what is going to replace it a few decades from now. But the Stoneys share this wealth among the community in a variety of ways, and a sizeable portion is invested for the future in terms of revenue and employment creating projects. Another portion is regularly being distributed among the population on a per capita basis and has served to make the Stoneys independent from the government's social assistance programs. Some might argue that these payments create the same syndrome as the welfare system - payment without gainful employment -, but for the people there is a crucial difference between the traditional sharing of a communally owned natural resource and the perpetuation of dependence on a paternalistic government. On the other hand it cannot be denied that these payments have served to curb economic activities, be it handicraft production (for the market) or realization of available employment opportunities at band enterprises like the ranch, the sawmill or the restaurant. This may simply be "human nature", but it must not be forgotten that like other tribes, the Stoneys look back at a long "welfare tradition" which is not easily overcome.

The Peigan are engaged in a desperate struggle to break away from their almost total dependence on the federal government, but they are caught in a vicious circle. Without the creation of more and/or larger economic enterprises they cannot raise more investment capital, but for the establishment of economic projects they depend on a government that is prepared to pool millions of dollars into social assistance but only a token sum into economic development. Therefore, so much depends for the Peigan on the settlement of land claims and water-related agreements. This situation puts this tribe under much more pressure than the Stoneys are exposed to, and makes it even more difficult to realize any degree of true "self-government". It also limits the scope for experimentation with alternative ways of socio-economic development.

The question of exactly how certain cultural traits and economic development accommodate each other, still lacks a conclusive answer. It is impossible to arrive at any generalizations. In both tribes there is the effort to channel incoming capital to the wider community in various ways, be it per capita distribution or investment in economic development projects such as the cow-calf program of the Peigan or the sawmill of the Stoneys. They also try to alleviate social problems by creating outlets for recreational and cultural needs such as the new community complex in Brocket or a future plan for Morley, an "Agriplex" for rodeo events. While the accumulation of capital is not a value in itself, nowadays money is needed and desired for the necessities of life and for other things native people have come to appreciate. Whether a tribal enterprise is competitive in the outside world or not, in the long run (though not at the experimental stage) it will have to be able to sustain itself, unless the tribe is in a position to subsidize it permanently. Thanks to their income in royalties the Stoneys have experienced more freedom than the Peigan to experiment and to do things in their own way. By means of traditional sharing mechanisms they have offset resource shortages in some areas such as land and embarked upon a variety of economic projects while trying to accommodate their people's cultural traits and needs. Many developments here are too recent to offer any conclusions.

Nevertheless, after looking at these two reserves, it appears that the idea of tribal homelands is a feasible one, even in terms of economic viability. The Stoneys have reached this goal for the time being thanks to the riches beneath their land, and the Peigan could achieve it too, if they were given a fair chance at economic development and if their substantial land claims were settled in a just manner.

While in many ways the two reserves are unique, they also illustrate a worldwide phenomenon: that of underdevelopment. Underdevelopment has been defined in a variety of ways:
"Taking the words literally, there is the obvious interpretation of underdeveloped - the natural resources have not been developed to the full extent possible" (Stamp 1960: 174 f).
"... an area where the natural resources are not developed or used to the best account, usually through lack of capital, technological backwardness and absence of stimulus" (Monkhouse 1965: 319).
Both definitions base their characterization of an underdeveloped area on the intensity of natural resource utilization. This type of definition also contains the implicit or even explicit assumption that maximum exploitation of natural resources is desirable. In contrast Myint (1958: 106) offers us a more differentiated approach. He, too, applies the terms "developed/underdeveloped" to natural resources but adds the terms "backward/economically advanced" which are meant to apply to the people of a given area: "The problem of the so-called 'underdeveloped countries' consists not merely in the 'underdevelopment' of their resources in the usual sense, but also in the economic 'backwardness' of their peoples. Where it exists, the 'underdevelopment' of natural resources and the 'backwardness' of people mutually aggravate each other in a 'vicious circle'." This definition places much more emphasis on the socio-economic character of the phenomenon than the other two definitions and provides us with a better starting-point to consider the complexity of the problem.

Therefore, we have to answer two questions with regard to the Stoney and Peigan Reserves:

a)   Are the natural resources of the reserves "underdeveloped", or are they utilized to their full potential?

b)   Can the Stoneys and Peigan be considered as "economically backward"?

The problem with these questions lies in their narrow conceptual framework. Turning to question a) and investigating the meaning of "underdeveloped resources" more closely, we find that in the language of optimum theory it describes two types of deviation (ibid.: 97 f):
i) less than optimum amounts of these "underdeveloped" resources have been used in producing final output
ii) less than optimum amounts of capital have been invested to augment the quantity and improve the quality of these "underdeveloped" resources.

As a rule these two types of deviation occur simultaneously, the first caused by the second. This is to say the scope for a more productive reorganization of "development" of all the resources of the underdeveloped area is limited without first removing the basic cause of "underdevelopment", i.e. an insufficient flow of investment. When we look at the southern Albertan Indian reserves though, we find that the degree of natural resource development tells us very little about the economic state of affairs of the areas concerned. Taking the Peigan Indians' agricultural land as an example, it is obvious that these lands are being utilized to almost their full capacity, with 75 per cent thereof being broken and optimum capital investment being realized for the most part. But because the land is leased out to off-reserve operators the community owning and depending on the resource only reaps a minor portion of the benefit. Likewise, the Stoneys' forests and rangeland were more fully utilized (and sometimes overused) before the onset of self-government than today, as they were managed by non-Indian ranchers and foresters, but the Indian occupants of the land were much more economically depressed than they are at present. The more salient question to ask is whether best use is made of the Indian resources to satisfy the communities' needs, or at least those needs that can be met by economic well-being as previously (see Chapter 4) defined:

> Economic well-being does not necessarily mean a high standard of living or great wealth, but rather freedom from want achieved through meaningful activity. It means having available and being able to choose from the widest possible range of options respecting lifestyle (National Indian Brotherhood 1977: 83).

The previous chapters have shown that a chronic shortage of investment capital on the Peigan Reserve stands in the way not only of a more intensive development of the reserve's natural resources but also of a community needs oriented utilization. With regard to land the very shortage of the resource itself in conjunction with social and historical realities is an obstacle to both a utilization that is either economically feasible or socially desirable. Among the Stoneys the shortage of land is somehow offset by their wealth in a non-renewable resource, gas. Their income from this source affords them the option of engaging in activities such as ranching in a way that may not seem economically feasible to an outsider but which certainly appears socially desirable to the Stoneys. It even enables them to bypass job opportunities and - the accumulation of capital not being part of their value system - makes them conduct business in a rather relaxed and informal manner that tends to baffle non-Indians. Thus the question whether the reserves' natural resources are "underdeveloped" can neither be answered with a "yes" or "no", nor is it really relevant.

The problem of economic backwardness is equally complex. This term, too, calls for a frame of reference which is western industrial society. Myint (ibid.: 115) observes two distinct aspects of this phenomenon: "On the subjective side it might be described as the economics of discontent and maladjustment; on the objective side it might be described as the economics of stagnation, low per capita productivity and incomes." One is not necessarily a counterpart of the other. Looking at traditional native culture(s), in spite of low productivity and lack of economic "progress", there was no problem of economic discontent and frustration; wants and activities were on the whole adapted to each other and the people were in equilibrium with their environment. This is not to say that everything was idyllic: There may have been frequent tribal wars and insecurity of life and property. But on the whole it is fair to say that there was no "problem" of backwardness in the modern sense. Backwardness in the sense of economic discontent and maladjustment does usually not fully emerge until the natural resources of "backward" peoples have been "developed" to a large extent, usually by foreign private enterprise, and the "backward" peoples have been partly converted to or forced into the new ways of life.

With regard to the Peigan and Stoneys objective characteristics generally associated with backward/underdeveloped areas have already been identified: young population, high dependency ratio, low per capita productivity and income, low degree of urbanization etc. But the subjective aspect in the sense of a discrepancy between human needs and the means to fulfill them equally applies. Concurrent with the settlement of the west the Peigan and Stoneys did not only witness the "development" of their natural resources beyond recognition but were also confined to small parcels of land and deprived of much more than their physical livelihood. Ever since and much more so than developing countries on a macro-scale they have been involved in a relationship of dependence with an immigrant society coupled with a strong element of conflict. They also have been unable to satisfy newly arising consumer needs conditioned by a new way of life they had been compelled to accept, and they have been denied the opportunity of managing their own affairs.

All these characteristics as well as the developments that created them are strongly reminiscent of the colonial scene in other parts of the world. The conceptualization of Indian reserves as internal colonies exploited by the dominant white group has been suggested by authors like Carstens (1971), Palmer Patterson (1972) and Frideres (1974). Subjection and dispossession, colonial administration and the creation of puppet political structures, degrees of assimilation or acculturation, renaissance and Pan-Indianism or the resurgence of tribal identity are colonial experiences familiar to the Stoneys and Peigan. For them the colonial experience as such has been compounded by the creation of a welfare syndrome. Among a people who have become more or less accustomed to a low subsistence level of living, subsistence from welfare can permanently replace subsistence from work, particularly where as in the case of many poor Indian bands, the work available for the members is often arduous, disagreeable and low paid, as in unskilled farm labour and construction jobs. Economic development under these circumstances faces special difficulties due to widespread apathy, resignation and lack of motivation.

The colonial experience cannot be undone, but it can be terminated. This will only happen when reserves cease to be treated as hinterlands - geographical and social areas to be exploited. There is some indication that this is gradually happening, but the means at the disposal of the poorer Indian bands such as the Peigan to realize their own brand of progress are still totally inadequate.

The National Indian Brotherhood (1977) identifies five Indian socio-economic development goals: the preservation of a cultural identity, achievement of economic well-being, a satisfying social milieu, the retention of the landbase and the "post-industrial society goal". The fifth goal is implicit in all four of the other goals, and is the opportunity to achieve these goals without necessarily being forced totally into the standard industrial mold. Thus we may conclude with the NIB (p. 80) that

> ... the course of socio-economic development for Indian people is not only a pressing question for an ethnic group but may well be important in the search, by all Canadians, for the good life as they enter the post-industrial era - an era in which the emphasis will be on conservation rather than consumption, on decentralization from large cities and an era which will cater to social man rather than economic man.

Bibliography

Agarwala, A.N., and Singh, S.P., eds., 1958, The Economics of Underdevelopment. Bombay, New York: Oxford University Press.

Agricultural Institute of Canada, 1969, The Agricultural Potential of Land on Indian Reserves. Agricultural Institute Review Jan.-Feb. 1969, pp. 23-26.

Agrisearch Investment Analysis Limited, 1977, Stoney Tribal Agricultural Ranching Project. Agrisearch Project No. A 115, Calgary.

Alberta Department of Agriculture, 1978, Management and Improvement of Rangeland. Agdex 134/14-7, May 1978.

Alberta Department of Lands and Forests, Lands Division, 1970, Range, its Nature and Use. Publication No. 146.

Anderson, E.W., 1967, Grazing Systems as Methods of Managing the Range Resources. Journal of Range Management 20, pp. 383-388.

— 1968, Soil Information for Range Resource Evaluation. Journal of Range Management 21, pp. 406-409.

Ashwell, I.Y., no date, Climatic Hazards on the Canadian Prairies. Unpublished Paper, University of Salford.

Bailey, A.W., and Wroe, R.A., 1974, Aspen Invasion in a Portion of the Alberta Parklands. Journal of Range Management 27, pp. 263-266.

Bailey, R.H., 1964, Report on the Forest Survey of the Stoney Indian Reserves Nos. 142, 143, and 144. Indian Reserve Forest Survey Report No. 14, Dept. of Forestry and Rural Development, Services Section, Ottawa, June 2, 1964.

Bank of Nova Scotia, 1978, Better Days for Canada's Forest Products. Monthly Review Nov.-Dec. 1978.

Baumgartner, D.M., ed., 1973, Management of Lodgepole Pine Ecosystems. Symposium Proceedings Vol. 1 & 2, held at Washington State University 9-11 Oct. 1973.

Beaty, C.B., 1972, Geomorphology, Geology, and Non-Agricultural Resources, pp. 11-19, in Jankunis, F., ed., 1972, Southern Alberta. A Regional Perspective. Lethbridge: University of Lethbridge.

Bell, D., 1976, The Coming of Post-Industrial Society. London: Basic Books.

Blanckenburg, P. van, and Schulz, M., 1970, The Socio-Economic Context of Agricultural Innovation Processes. Zeitschrift für ausländische Landwirtschaft 9, pp. 317-332.

Calgary Urban Treaty Indian Alliance, no date, The Calgary Urban Treaty Indian Alliance (CUTIA). Unpublished Paper, Calgary.

Bonnor, G.M., 1969, Report on the Forest Survey of the Bighorn Indian Reserve No. 144A. Indian Reserve Forest Survey Report No. 28, Canada Department of Fisheries and Forestry, Ottawa, Dec. 1969.

Bowles, R.T., 1979, Social Impact Assessment in small Canadian Communities. Peterborough: Trent University.

Bowser, W.E., 1960, The Soils of the Prairies. Agricultural Institute Review March-April 1960, pp. 24-26.

Brayshaw, T.C., 1965, Key to the Native Trees of Canada. Ottawa: Department of Forestry.

Budd, A.C., 1952, A Key to Plants of the Farming and Ranching Areas of the Canadian Prairies. Experimental Farm Service, Department of Agriculture.

Calgary Urban Treaty Indian Alliance (CUTIA), no date, Indians in Canadian Society and the Calgary Urban Treaty Indian Alliance.

Campbell, J.B., et al, 1962, Range Management of Grasslands and Adjacent Parklands in the Prairie Provinces. Canada Department of Agriculture, Research Branch, Publication No. 1133.

Campbell, K.P., 1976, An Analysis and Report on the Potential for the Stoney Sawmill at Morley, Alberta, July 1976.

Canada Department of Agriculture, 1968, Cattle Ranching in Southern Alberta. Regina: Economics Branch, Febr. 1968.

Carder, A.C., 1970, Climate and Rangelands of Canada, Journal of Range Management 23, pp. 263-267.

Cardinal, H., 1969, The Unjust Society. Edmonton: M.G. Hurtig.

— 1977, The Rebirth of Canada's Indians. Edmonton: M.G. Hurtig.

— 1978, Treaties Six and Seven: The Next Century, pp. 132-138 in Getty, I.A.L., and Smith, D.B., eds., 1978, One Century Later. Western Canadian Reserve Indians since Treaty 7. Vancouver: University of British Columbia Press.

Carlson, N.R., 1980, Mineral Potential (other than Oil and Natural Gas) of Peigan No. 147 and Peigan No. 147B Indian Reserves. Department of Indian and Northern Affairs, Indian Mineral (West). Calgary, February 1980.

Carstens, W., 1971, Coercion and Change, pp. 120-132 in Ossenberg, R.J., ed., 1971, Canadian Society: Pluralism, Change, and Conflict. Scarborough: Prentice-Hall.

Colton, H.W., 1967, Livestock Grazing under Multiple-Use Policy. Journal of Range Management 20, pp. 113-114.

Coupland, R.T., 1958, The Effects of Fluctuations in Weather upon the Grasslands of the Great Plains. The Botanical Review 24, pp. 274-315.

— 1961, A Reconsideration of Grassland Classification in the Northern Great Plains of North America. Journal of Ecology 49, pp. 135-167.

Couture, J.E., 1978, Philosophy and Psychology of Native Education, pp. 126-131 in Getty, I.A.L., and Smith, D.B., eds., 1978, One Century Later. Western Canadian Reserve Indians since Treaty 7. Vancouver: University of British Columbia Press.

Cox, B., ed., 1973, Cultural Ecology. Readings on the Canadian Indians and Eskimos. Toronto: McClelland Steward.

Crown, P.H., 1977, Another Look at Strip Farming in Southern Alberta. Agriculture and Forestry Bulletin Fall 1977, University of Alberta, pp. 3-5.

Cumming, P.A., and Mickenberg, N.H., eds., 1972, Native Rights in Canada. The Indian-Eskimo Association of Canada in association with General Publishing Company Limited, Toronto.

Cuthand, S., 1978, The Native Peoples of the Prairie Provinces in the 1920s and 1930s, pp. 31-41 in Getty, I.A.L., and Smith, D.B., eds., 1978, One Century Later. Western Canadian Reserve Indians since Treaty 7. Vancouver: University of British Columbia Press.

Daniel, R.C., 1980, A History of Native Claims Processes in Canada, 1867-1979, prepared by R.C. Daniel, Tyler, Wright & Daniel Limited, Research Consultants for Research Branch, Department of Indian and Northern Affairs. February 1980.

Davis, A.K., ed., 1967, A Northern Dilemma 1. Reference Papers. Washington, Bellingham.

— 1968, Urban Indians in Western Canada: Implications for Social Theory and Social Policy. Transactions of the Royal Society of Canada, Volume 6, Series 4, June 1968, pp. 217-228.

Dealy, J., 1973, Management of Lodgepole Pine Ecosystems for Range and Wildlife, pp. 556-568 in Baumgartner, D.M., ed., 1973, Management of Lodgepole Pine Ecosystems. Symposium Proceedings Vol. 1 & 2, held at Washington State University 9-11 Oct. 1973.

Deloria, V. Jr., 1969, Custer Died for your Sins. An Indian Manifesto. New York: Avon.

Dempsey, H.A., 1972, Crowfoot. Chief of the Blackfeet. Edmonton: Hurtig Publishers.

— 1978a, Indian Tribes of Alberta. Calgary: Glenbow-Alberta Institute.

— 1978b, Charcoal's World. Saskatoon: Western Producer Prairie Books.

— 1978c, One Hundred Years of Treaty Seven, pp. 20-30 in Getty I.A.L., and Smith, D.B., eds., 1978, One Century Later. Western Canadian Reserve Indians since Treaty 7. Vancouver: University of British Columbia Press.

— 1980, Red Crow. Warrior Chief. Saskatoon: Western Producer Prairie Books.

Deprez, P., and Sigurdson, G., 1969, The Economic Status of the Canadian Indian. Centre for Settlement Studies, University of Manitoba, Series 2: Research Report No. 1.

— no date, The economic Status of the Indian Reserves: A Case of Underdevelopment or Regional Disparity. Unpublished Research Paper, Winnipeg: University of Manitoba.

Downs, J., 1973, Comments on Plains Indian Cultural Development, pp. 171-173 in Cox, B., ed., 1973, Cultural Ecology. Readings on the Canadian Indians and Eskimos. Toronto: McClelland Steward.

Dunning, R.W., 1974, Some Problems of Reserve Indian Communities: A Case Study, pp. 59-85 in Frideres, J.S., ed., 1974, Canada's Indians. Contemporary Conflicts. Scarborough: Prentice-Hall of Canada Ltd.

D & S Petroleum Consultants Ltd., 1974, An Evaluation of the Interests of the Stoney Nation in the Jumping Pound West Field. Calgary, April 1974.

Edwards, N., 1961/62, Economic Development of Indian Reserves. Human Organization 20, Winter 1961/62, pp. 197-202.

Ehrlich, W.A., and Odynsky, W.M., 1960, Soils developed under Forest in the Great Plains Region. Agricultural Institute Review March-April 1960, pp. 29-32.

Elgaard, K., 1968, Cattle Ranching in Southern Alberta. Family operated commercial Cattle Ranches. Foothills and Shortgrass Regions. Regina: Canada Department of Agriculture, Economics Branch.

England, R.E., 1966, A Partial Study of the Resource Potential of the Stoney Indian Reservation: Livestock and Forest Enterprises. Unpublished M.A. Thesis, Department of Geography, University of Calgary.

England, R.E., and De Vos, A., 1969, Influence of Animals on Pristine Conditions on the Canadian Grasslands. Journal of Range Management 22, pp. 87-94.

Ewers, J.C., 1955, The Horse in Blackfoot Indian Culture, Washington: Smithsonian Institution. Bureau of American Ethnology, Bulletin 159.

— 1958, The Blackfeet. Raiders of the Northwestern Plains. University of Oklahoma Press.

Federation of Saskatchewan Indians, 1977, The Indian Right to Education. November 1977.

— 1978, The Indian Act, the Constitution, Indian Treaties and Indian Government. A Position Paper. July 1978.

— 1978, Indian Economic Development. A Draft Discussion Paper. August 1978.

Fisher, A.D., 1974, Introducing "Our Betrayed Wards", by R.N. Wilson. Western Canadian Journal of Anthropology 4, No. 2, pp. 21-31.

— 1973, The Algonquian Plains? pp. 174-188 in Cox, B., ed., 1973, Cultural Ecology. Readings on the Canadian Indians and Eskimos. Toronto: McClelland and Stewart.

Fisher, R., 1977, Contact and Conflict. Indian-European Relations in British Columbia, 1774-1890. Vancouver: University of British Columbia Press.

Fletcher, R.J., 1972, The Climate of Southern Alberta, pp. 20-34 in Jankunis, F., ed., 1972, Southern Alberta. A Regional Perspective. Lethbridge: University of Lethbridge.

Foster, J.E., 1979, Indian-White Relations in the Prairie West during the Fur Trade Period - A Compact, pp. 181-200 in Price, R., ed., The Spirit of the Alberta Indian Treaties. Toronto: Butterworth & Co. (Canada) Ltd.

Frideres, J.S., ed., 1974, Canada's Indians. Contemporary Conflicts. Scarborough: Prentice-Hall of Canada Ltd.

Getty, I.A.L., and Larner, J.W., 1972, The Kootenay Plains and the Big Horn Wesley Stoney Band - An Oral and Documentary Historical Study, 1800-1970. Unpublished Research Report, Morley: Stoney Tribal Council.

Getty, I.A.L., and Smith, D.B., eds., 1978, One Century Later. Western Canadian Reserve Indians since Treaty 7. Vancouver: University of British Columbia Press.

Getty, W.E.A., 1974, Perception as an Agent of sociocultural Change for the Stoney Indians of Alberta. Unpublished M.A. Thesis, Department of Anthropology, University of Calgary.

Getty, W.E.A., 1975, A Case History and Analysis of Stoney Indian-Governmental Interaction with Regard to the Bighorn Dam: The Effects of Citizen Participation - A Lesson on Government Perfidy and Indian Frustration. Unpublished M.S.W. Thesis, Faculty of Social Welfare, University of Calgary.

Gibbins, R., and Ponting, J.R., 1978, Prairie Canadians' Orientations towards Indians, pp. 82-102 in Getty, I.A.L., and Smith, D.B., eds., 1978, One Century Later. Western Canadian Reserve Indians since Treaty 7. Vancouver: University of British Columbia Press.

Goldfrank, E.S., 1945, Changing Configurations in the Social Organization of a Blackfoot Tribe during the Reserve Period. New York: J.J.Augustin.

Government of Canada, 1969, Statement of the Government of Canada on Indian Policy 1969 ("White Paper"). Presented to the First Session of the 28th Parliament by the Honourable Jean Chretien, Minister of Indian Affairs and Northern Development.

Greenfield, S.F., 1967, Water Requirements for Improved Livestock Performance on Rangeland. Journal of Range Management 20, pp. 333-334.

Grier, N., and McGregor, A.K., 1977, Basic Plan for Agriculture, Peigan Reserve. Brocket: Peigan Tribal Administration.

Hamre, V., 1973, Management for Multiple Use, pp. 651-657 in Baumgartner, D.M., ed., 1973, Management of Lodgepole Pine Ecosystems. Symposium Proceedings Vol. 1 & 2, held at Washington State University 9-11 Oct. 1973.

Harbeck, W., 1973, The Stoney Cultural Education Program. A Paper delivered at the Northern Cross-Cultural Education Symposium: Needs and Resources. University of Alaska, Fairbanks, Nov. 8, 1973.

Havighurst, R.J., 1972, Education among American Indians: Individual and Cultural Aspects, pp. 89-102 in Nagler, M., ed., 1972, Perspectives on the Northamerican Indians. Toronto: McClelland and Stewart.

Hawthorn, H.B., ed., 1966, A Survey of the Contemporary Indians of Canada, Two Volumes. Ottawa: Indian Affairs Branch.

Heady, H.F., 1970, Grazing Systems: Terms and Definitions. Journal of Range Management 23, pp. 59-61.

Herrington, R.B., 1973, Recreational Problems and Opportunities of Lodgepole Pine, pp. 581-587 in Baumgartner, D.M., ed., 1973, Management of Lodgepole Pine Ecosystems. Symposium Proceedings Vol. 1 & 2, held at Washington State University 9-11 Oct. 1973.

Hicks, O.N., 1970, The First American and his Range Resource. Journal of Range Management 23, pp. 391-396.

Hilton, J.E., and Bailey, A.W., 1974, Forage Production and Utilization in a Sprayed Aspen Forest in Alberta. Journal of Range Management 27, pp. 375-380.

Hodge, F.W., 1913, Handbook of Indians of Canada. Ottawa: C.H. Parmelee King's Printer.

Holmes, A., 1965, Principles of Physical Geology. 2nd revised edition. London: Thomas Nelson and Sons Ltd.

Hosie, R.C., 1969, Native Trees of Canada. Ottawa: Canadian Forestry Service, Department of the Environment.

Howard, L., 1979, Social Impact Assessment - The Bighorn and High Arrow Dams in Retrospect. Unpublished M.E.D. Thesis, Faculty of Environmental Design, University of Calgary.

Indian Affairs, 1889, Description and Plans of certain Indian Reserves in the Province of Manitoba and the Northwest Territories 1889. Indian Reserve Plans, Ottawa.

— 1966, The Canadian Indian. A Reference Paper. Indian Affairs Branch, Department of Indian Affairs and Northern Development. Ottawa.

— 1967, Indians of the Prairie Provinces. A Historical Review. Indian Affairs Branch, Department of Indian Affairs and Northern Development. Ottawa.

— 1969, History of Government. Indian Policy. Department of Indian Affairs and Northern Development. Ottawa.

— 1980, Indian Conditions. A Survey. Indian and Northern Affairs Canada. Ottawa.

— no date, Legal Aspects of Economic Development on Indian Reserve Lands. Indian and Eskimo Affairs Program, Economic Development Operations.

Indian Association of Alberta, no date, Economic Development and the Spirit of the Treaties. Treaty and Aboriginal Rights Research (TARR) of the Indian Association of Alberta. Edmonton.

— 1977, Joint NIB/DIAND Socio-Economic Study for Alberta Region. Submitted by the Indian Association of Alberta, March 31, 1977.

Indian Chiefs of Alberta, 1970, Citizen Plus ("Red Paper"). A Presentation by the Indian Chiefs of Alberta to Right Honourable P.E. Trudeau, Prime Minister and the Government of Canada. June 1970.

James, B.J., 1972, Continuity and Emergence in Indian Poverty Culture, pp. 227-240 in Nagler, M., ed., 1972, Perspectives on the Northamerican Indians. Toronto: McClelland Steward.

Jankunis, F., ed., 1972, Southern Alberta. A Regional Perspective. Lethbridge: University of Lethbridge.

Jenness, D., 1932, Indians of Canada. Ottawa: National Museum of Canada, Anthropological Series No. 15.

— 1954, Canada's Indians Yesterday, What of Today? Canadian Journal of Economics and Political Science 20, pp. 95-100.

Johnston, A., and Wilson, D.B., 1962, The Range Story of the Prairies. Agricultural Institute Review Jan.-Feb. 1962, pp. 9-11, p. 41.

— Smoliak, S., and Slen, S.B., 1966, Trends in Livestock Population of the Canadian Prairies. Agricultural Institute Review July-Aug. 1966, pp. 10-12.

— and Smoliak, S., 1968, Reclaiming Brushland in Southwestern Alberta. Journal of Range Management 21, pp. 404-406.

— 1970, A History of the Rangelands of Western Canada. Journal of Range Management 23, pp. 3-8.

— Dormaar, J.F., and Smoliak, S., 1971, Long-Term Grazing Effects on Fescue Grassland Soils. Journal of Range Management 24, pp. 185-188.

Johnston, A., Dormaar, J.F., and Smoliak, S., 1972, Canada's Rangeland Resources - A Look Ahead. Journal of Range Management 25, pp. 333-338.

Jubenville, A., 1976, Outdoor Recreation Planning. Toronto: W.B. Saunders Company.

Kennedy, D. (Ochankugahe), 1972, Recollections of an Assiniboine Chief. Edited and with an Introduction by J.R. Stevens. Toronto: McClelland and Stewart.

Kumar, P., 1976, Forest Management Plan, Stoney Indian Reserve 142B (Rabbit Lake). Edmonton: Department of Indian Affairs and Northern Development.

— 1977, Forest Management on the Indian Reserves. Agriculture and Forestry Bulletin Fall 1977, University of Alberta, pp. 34-37.

Kupfer, G., and Langin, R., 1978, Oldman River Basin Study. Phase II. Social Impact Assessment. P. Boothroyd & Co-West-Associates, June 1978.

Lagasse, J.H., 1961/62, Community Development in Manitoba. Human Organization 20, 4, pp. 232-237.

Larner, J.W. Jr., 1976, The Kootenay Plains Land Question and Canadian Indian Policy, 1799-1949: A Synopsis. The Western Canadian Journal of Anthropology 4, No. 2, pp. 83-92.

Laurie, J., no date, Truce between the Kootenays and the Stoneys. John Laurie Papers, File 22, unpublished Manuscript, Glenbow Public Archives, Calgary.

— 1957-59, The Stoney Indians of Alberta, Vol. 1. Glenbow Foundation, Calgary.

Leakey, A., 1961, The Soils of Canada from a pedological Viewpoint, pp. 147-157 in Legget, R.F., ed., Soils in Canada. Toronto: University of Toronto Press.

— 1967, The Canada Land Inventory. Its Significance to Agricultural Land Use Planning. Agricultural Institute Review Nov.-Dec. 1967, pp. 18-20.

Legget, R.F., ed., 1961, Soils in Canada. Toronto: University of Toronto Press.

Lewis, O., 1941, The Effects of White Contact upon Blackfoot Culture with special Reference to the Role of the Fur Trade. Monographs of the American Ethnological Society No. 6, Seattle and London: University of Washington Press.

Lodge, R.W., 1970, Complementary Grazing Systems for the Northern Great Plains. Journal of Range Management 23, pp. 268-271.

— et al, 1971, Management of the Western Range. Canada Department of Agriculture, Publication No. 1425.

— Smoliak, S., and Johnston, A., 1972, Managing Crested Wheatgrass Pastures. Canada Department of Agriculture, Publication No. 1473.

Lombard North Group & Sibbald Group, 1978, Environmental Overview of selected on-stream and off-stream storage sites in the Oldman River Basin, Vol. 1. June 1978.

Lowie, R.H., 1909, The Assiniboine. New York: Anthropological Papers of the American Museum of Natural History, Vol. 4.

MacEwan, G., 1969, Tatanga Mani. Walking Buffalo of the Stoneys. Edmonton: Hurtig Publishers.

— 1971, Portraits from the Plains. Toronto: McGraw-Hill Company of Canada Limited.

MacGregor, G., 1961/62, Community Development and Social Adaptation. Human Organization 20, 4, pp. 238-242.

MacGregor, J.G., 1954, Behold the Shining Mountains. Being an Account of the Travels of Anthony Henday, 1754-55, the first white Man to enter Alberta. Edmonton: Applied Art Products.

Maclean, J., 1927, McDougall of Alberta. Toronto: Ryerson Press.

Manuel, G., and Posluns, M., 1974, The Fourth World. Don Mills, Ont.: Collier-Macmillan Canada.

Manyfingers, W., 1979, Indian Government and the Treaties. Paper given at the All Chiefs' Conference, Calgary, March 19-23, 1979.

Marule, M. Smallface, 1978, The Canadian Government's Termination Policy: From 1969 to the Present Day, pp. 103-116 in Getty, I.A.L., and Smith, D.B., eds., 1978, One Century Later. Western Canadian Reserve Indians since Treaty 7. Vancouver: University of British Columbia Press.

Marv Anderson & Associates Limited, Agro-Economic Consultants, 1978, Oldman River Basin Study, Phase II. Economic Analysis of Water Supply Alternatives. April 1978.

McClintock, W., 1910, The Old North Trail. London: Macmillan.

McHugh, T., 1972, The Time of the Buffalo. Lincoln and London: University of Nebraska Press.

McNickle, A., 1961/62, Private Intervention. Human Organization 20,4, pp. 208-215.

McQuillan, D.A., 1980, Creation of Indian Reserves on the Canadian Prairies 1870-1885. The Geographical Review 70, 4, pp. 379-396.

Monkhouse, F.J., 1965, A Dictionary of Geography. Chicago: Aldine Pub. Co.

Morgan, W.B., and Munton R.J.C., 1971, Agricultural Geography. London: Methuen and Co. Limited.

Morris, A., 1880 (1971), The Treaties of Canada with the Indians of Manitoba and the Northwest Territories, including the Negotiations on which they were based, and other Information relating thereto. Toronto: Willing & Williamson.

Moss, E.M., 1932, The Vegetation of Alberta: The Poplar Association and Related Vegetation of Central Alberta. Journal of Ecology 20, pp. 380-415.

— and Campbell, J.A., 1947, The Fescue Grassland of Alberta. Canadian Journal of Reserarch 25, pp. 209-227.

— 1955, The Vegetation of Alberta. The Botanical Review 21, pp. 507-525.

Munroe, S.W., 1969, Warriors of the Rock: Basic Social Structure of the Mountain Bands of Stoney Indians at Morley, Alberta. Unpublished M.A. Thesis, Department of Anthropology, University of Calgary.

Myint, H., 1958, An Interpretation of Economic Backwardness, pp. 92-132, in Agarwala, A.N., and Singh, S.P., eds., 1958, The Economics of Underdevelopment. Bombay, New York: Oxford University Press.

Nagler, M., ed., 1972, Perspectives on the Northamerican Indians. Toronto: McClelland and Stewart.

National Indian Brotherhood (NIB), 1972, Indian Economic Development: A Whiteman's Whitewash. Unpublished Paper, Oct. 1972, Ottawa.

— 1975, Statement on the Role of Tourism and Outdoor Recreation for rural Development as it applies to Indian People and Indian Lands to the Canadian Council on Rural Development by the National Indian Brotherhood. Ottawa, Nov. 25-28, 1975.

— 1977, A Strategy for the Socio-Economic Development of Indian People. Background Report No. 1, Ottawa, Sept. 1977.

Neils, E.M., 1971, Reservation to City. University of Chicago, Department of Geography, Research Paper No. 131.

Newton, J.D., 1971, Story of Irrigation Development in Alberta and Notes on Irrigation in the Far East. Edmonton: University of Alberta.

Nix, J.E., 1960, Mission among the Buffalo: The Labours of the Reverends George M. and John C. McDougall in the Canadian Northwest, 1860-1876. Toronto: Ryerson Press.

Norris, D.K., and Bally, A.W., 1972, Coal, Oil, Gas and Industrial Mineral Deposits of the Interior Plains, Foothills and Rocky Mountains of Alberta and British Columbia. Excursions A 25- C 25 Guide, 24. International Geological Congress, Montreal 1972.

O'Hara, W.F.T., et al., 1975, Stoney Indian Park, Morley, Alberta, Project No. 2-9-117, Department of Indian Affairs and Northern Development.

O'Malley, M., 1976, The Past and Future Land. An Account of the Berger Inquiry into the Mackenzie Valley Pipeline. Toronto: Peter Martin Associates Limited.

Ossenberg, R.J., ed., 1971, Canadian Society: Pluralism, Change, and Conflict. Scarborough: Prentice-Hall.

Palmer Patterson, E., 1972, The Canadian Indian: A History Since 1500. Don Mills, Ont.: Collier-Macmillan Canada.

Pelletier, W., 1971, For every North American Indian who begins to disappear I also begin to disappear. Toronto: Neewin Publishing Company Limited.

Philipps Petroleum Company Western Hemisphere, 1980, Application to the Energy Resources Conservation Board for Approval to construct the Ghost River Gas Plant. Calgary, Dec. 1980.

Ponting, J.R., and Gibbins, R., 1980, Out of Irrelevance. A socio-political introduction to Indian affairs in Canada. Toronto: Butterworth and Company (Canada) Limited.

Powderface, S., 1974, Stoney Band's Current Attitudes, Perceptions, Aspirations and Expectations. Study Report to the Stoney Cultural Education Program, Nov. 1974.

Price, F.E., 1967, An Evaluation of the Potential of the Peigan Indian Reserve. Frank E. Price & Associates Ltd. March 1967.

Price, J., and McCaskill, D.N., 1974, The Urban Integration of Canadian Native People. Western Canadian Journal of Anthropology 4, 2, pp. 29-41.

Price, R., ed., 1979, The Spirit of the Alberta Indian Treaties. Toronto: Butterworth and Company (Canada) Limited.

Raczka, P.M., 1979, Winter Count. A History of the Blackfoot People. Calgary: Standard Book.

Ray, A., 1972, Indian Adaptations to the Forest-Grassland Boundary of Manitoba and Saskatchewan, 1650-1821: Some Implications for Interregional Migration. The Canadian Geographer 16, pp. 103-118.

—   1974, Indians in the Fur Trade; their Role as Trappers, Hunters, and Middlemen in the Lands Southwest of Hudson Bay, 1660-1870. Toronto: University of Toronto Press.

—   1978, Fur Trade History as an Aspect of Native History, pp. 7-19 in Getty, I.A.L., and Smith, D.B., eds., 1978, One Century Later. Western Canadian Reserve Indians since Treaty 7. Vancouver: University of British Columbia Press.

Rieber, J., 1981, Historical Time-Bombs. Calgary, April 1981, pp. 109-112.

Roe, F.G., 1934, The Extermination of the Buffalo in Western Canada. The Canadian Historical Review 15, pp. 1-23.

—   1955, The Indian and the Horse. University of Oklahoma Press.

Rowe, J.S., 1972, Forest Regions of Canada. Canadian Forestry Service Publication No. 1300, Department of Environment, Ottawa.

Rowe, T.K.L., et al., 1973, Management Consulting Services, Heritage/Stoney Wilderness School. Project No. 2-9-095, Department of Indian Affairs and Northern Development, Oct. 1973.

Ryan, J., 1978, Wall of Words. The Betrayal of the Urban Indian. Toronto: Peter Martin Associates Limited.

Satterlund, D.R., 1973, Climatic Factors and Lodgepole Pine, pp. 297-309 in Baumgartner, D.M., ed., 1973, Management of Lodgepole Pine Ecosystems. Symposium Proceedings Vol. 1 & 2, held at Washington State University 9-11 Oct. 1973.

Scott-Brown, J.M., Stoney Ethnobotany: An Indication of cultural Change amongst the Stoney of Morley, Alberta. Unpublished M.A. Thesis, Department of Anthropology, University of Calgary.

Siggner, A., and Locatelli, C., 1980, An Overview of demographic, social and economic Conditions among Alberta's registered Indian Population. Indian and Inuit Affairs Program, Research Branch, Edmonton, Jan. 1980.

Smoliak, S., 1968, Grazing Studies on Native Range, Crested Wheatgrass, and Russian Wildrye Pastures. Journal of Range Management 21, pp. 47-50.

—   Dormaar, J.F., and Johnston, A., 1972, Long-Term Grazing Effects on Stipa-Bouteloua Prairie Soils. Journal of Range Management 25, pp. 246-250.

—   and Slen, S.B., 1974, Beef Production of Native Range, Crested Wheatgrass, and Russian Wildrye Pastures. Journal of Range Management 27, pp. 433-436.

Smoliak, S., et al., 1976, Guide to Range Condition and Stocking Rates for Alberta. Edmonton: Alberta Energy and Natural Resources.

Snow, J., 1977, These Mountains are our Sacred Places. Toronto: Samuel-Stevens, Publishers.

Stamp, L.D., 1960, Our Developing World. London: Faber and Faber.

Steiner, S., 1968, The New Indians. New York: Harper and Row.

Stobbe, P.C., 1960, The Great Soil Groups of Canada. Agricultural Institute Review March-April 1960, pp. 20-22, p.26.

Stoddar, L.A., Smith, A.D., and Box, T.W., 1975, Range Management. 3rd edition. Toronto: Mc Graw-Hill Company of Canada Limited.

Synergy West Limited, Consultants, 1975, 147B (Peigan Timber Limit). Calgary.

Taylor, J.L., 1979, Canada's Northwest Indian Policy in the 1870s: Traditional Premises and Necessary Innovations, pp. 3-7 in Price, R., ed., 1979, The Spirit of the Alberta Indian Treaties. Toronto: Butterworth & Co. (Canada) Ltd.

— 1979, Two Views on the Meaning of Treaties Six and Seven, pp. 9-45 in Price, R., ed., 1979, The Spirit of the Alberta Indian Treaties. Toronto: Butterworth & Co (Canada) Ltd.

Telfer, E.S., and Scotter, G.W., 1975, Potential for Game Ranching in Boreal Aspen Forests of Western Canada. Journal of Range Management 28, pp. 172-180.

Tobias, J.L., 1975, Indian Reserves in Western Canada: Indian Homelands or Devices for Assimilation, pp. 89-103 in Muise, D.A., ed., Approaches to Native History in Canada. Papers of a Conference held at the National Museum of Man, Ottawa 1975. Ottawa: National Museum of Canada, 1977.

— 1976, Protection, Civilization, Assimilation: An Outline History of Canada's Indian Policy. The Western Canadian Journal of Anthropology 6, 2, pp. 13-30.

Underwood McLellan and Associates Limited, 1969, Land Use Study, Stoney Indian Reserves (Morley, Eden Valley, Bighorn). Calgary.

— 1970, A Program for the Stoney People. Recreation Resource Study, Morley Indian Reserve. Calgary.

Upton, L.F.S., 1973, The Origins of Canadian Indian Policy. Journal of Canadian Studies 6, 4, pp. 51-61.

Vogt, E.Z., 1972, The Acculturation of American Indians, pp. 2-13 in Nagler, M., ed., 1972, Perspectives on the Northamerican Indians. Toronto: McClelland and Stewart.

Weaver, S.M., 1981, Making Canadian Indian Policy. The Hidden Agenda 1968-1970. Toronto: University of Toronto Press.

Western Research and Development Limited, 1975, Site Selection Study, Phase I, Environmental Impact Assessment. Proposed Morley-Ghost River Gas Plant. Calgary, August 1975.

— 1980, Site Selection Study and Environmental Impact Assessment for the Ghost River Gas Project. Calgary, October 1980.

Williams, J.W., 1955, First in the West. The Story of Henry Kelsey, Discoverer of the Canadian Prairies. Edmonton: Applied Art Products.

Wormington, H.M., 1965, An Introduction to the Archaeology of Alberta, Canada. Proceedings No. 11, Denver Museum of Natural History, Denver, Colorado.

Wright, H.A., 1974, Range Burning. Journal of Range Management 27, pp. 5-11.

Wroe, R.A., et al., 1979, Range Pastures in Alberta. ENR Report no. 86. Edmonton: Alberta Agriculture and Alberta Energy and Natural Resources.

Wuttunee, W.I.C., 1971, Ruffled Feathers. Indians in Canadian Society. Calgary: Bell Books Limited.

Wyatt, F.A., et al., 1943, Soil Survey of Rosebud and Banff Sheets. College of Agriculture, University of Alberta, Bulletin No. 40, July 1943.

Zentner, H., 1967, The Pre-Machine Ethic of the Athabascan-speaking Indians: Avenue or Barrier to Assimilation? pp. 70-89 in Davis A.K., ed., 1967, A Northern Dilemma 1. Reference Papers. Washington, Bellingham.

Official Documents: Annual Reports of the Department of Indian Affairs from 1880 to 1980

Indian Economic Development Direct Loan Order;
Indian Economic Development Guarantee Order.
Canada Gazette Part II Vol. 112 No. 1, pp. 198-209.

Indian Act, R.S., c. 1-6 amended by c.10 (2nd Supp.) 1974-75-76, c.48, 1978.

Copy of Treaty and Supplementary Treaty No. 7, made 22nd September and 4th December, 1977 between Her Majesty the Queen and the Blackfeet and other Indian Tribes, at the Blackfoot Crossing of Bow River and Fort Macleod 1877.
Reprinted 1966 from 1877, Ottawa: Queen's Printer.

Topographical Maps:
Peigan Reserves 1 : 250,000
Series A 502 Map 82 H Edition 3MCE

Peigan Reserves 1 : 50,000
Series A 741 Map 82H/5 Edition 2MCE
Series A 741 Map 82H/12 Edition 3MCE

Stoney Reserves 1 : 250,000
Series A 502 Map 82O Edition 2ASE
Series A 502 Map 83C Edition 1ASE
Series A 502 Map 82J Edition 2MCE

Stoney Reserves 1 : 50,000
Series A 741 Map 82O/2 Edition 2MCE
Series A 741 Map 82O/3 east Edition 1ASE
Series A 741 Map 82O/7 west Edition 1ASE
Series A 741 Map 82O/7 east Edition 2MCE
Series A 741 Map 83C/8 Edition 2MCE
Series A 741 Map 82J/7 east Edition 2MCE
Series A 741 Map 82J/8 Edition 2MCE

Canada Land Inventory Maps: Soil Capability for Agriculture 82O and 82H

                                Outdoor Recreation 82O and 82H

Aerial Photographs: Peigan Reserves 1970
                                A 21850 1-5
                                A 21735 23-25

                                Peigan Reserves 1973
                                A 23233 107-113
                                A 23233 230-236

                                Stoney Reserves 1972
                                A 23010 54-56
                                A 23010 141-144

                                Stoney Reserves 1975
                                A 24070 143-145
                                A 24069 159-170

                                Peigan Reserve 147:
                                Photomap compiled from 1980 vertical aerial photographs Roll No.
                                A 25569, Energy, Mines and Resources Canada 1981.

Newspapers: Calgary Herald
                                Kainai News
                                Lethbridge Herald
                                Nations' Ensign

1706566

Claudia Notzke: Indian Reserves in Canada

Gedruckt bei Wenzel